# CHILD LABOUR AND STREET CHILDREN
## *ISSUES AND CONCERNS*

# CHILD LABOUR
# AND
# STREET CHILDREN
## *ISSUES AND CONCERNS*

*Edited by*

**Prof. Yerroju Bhaskaracharyulu**

*Professor & Former Head of the Dept.*
*Dept. of Adult & Continuing Education*
*Andhra University*
*Visakhapatnam (Andhra Pradesh)*
*(India)*

*&*

**Dr. (Smt.) Yerroju Nirmala**

**DISCOVERY PUBLISHING HOUSE PVT. LTD.**
**NEW DELHI-110 002**

*Published by:*
**Tilak Wasan**

**DISCOVERY PUBLISHING HOUSE PVT. LTD.**
4383/4B, Ansari Road, Darya Ganj
New Delhi-110 002 (India)
*Phone* : +91-11-23279245, 43596064-65
*Fax* : +91-11-23253475
*E-mail* : discoverypublishinghouse@gmail.com
sales@discoverypublishinggroup.com
parul.wasan@gmail.com
*web* : www.discoverypublishinggroup.com

***First Edition:* 2014**

**ISBN: 978-93-5056-467-7**

**Child Labour and Street Children**
***Issues and Concerns***



*Printed at:*
Dynamic Printers
Delhi

# Preface

Children are often the most abused in the society. Their rights violated, their aspirations are ignored and their dreams fast dissolve. Despite progressive laws and court orders, millions of Indian boys and girls lead a nightmarish existence. About 200 million people still go to bed hungry. Government provisions of eradicating poverty are still as elusive as water in a desert. What is more, minimum wages and free education not only remain distant dreams to many but are, in a way, important reasons for child labour. India has followed a proactive policy in the matter of tackling the problems of child labour. India always stood for constitutional statutory and developmental measures required in eliminating child labour. The Indian constitution has consciously incorporated provisions to secure Compulsory Universal Elementary Education as well as labour protection for children. Labour commissions in India have gone into the problems of child labour and have made extensive recommendations.

In this context, an edited volume on **"Child Labour and Street Children:** ***Issues and Concerns*****"** has brought out for wider dissemination. This book consists of some selected papers were compiled and contributed by the distinguish scholars and academicians in this field. This book consists of 20 papers on the following themes.

1. Child Labour and Street Children: *Issues and Concerns*
2. Child Labour, Street Children and Education
3. Child Rights

The merit of this volume lies in a contemporary relevance of the subject and a vast variety of topics covered. Distinguished academicians and scholars from all over the country have contributed their wisdom in a logically arranged sequence and explained the theoretical and practical aspects in this field.

We believe that this book will be immensely significant and useful for the researchers and academicians in the field of Child Labour/Street Children Issues and concerns and this volume would prove immensely beneficial.

We are thankful to our colleagues and all other departments' personnel who associated with this task directly or indirectly. We are very much thankful to the contributors for their significant and scholarly contributions. Their choice of theme is relevant and it is the emergent need of the present age. All contributors deserve our appreciation for their contribution in producing this book.

We are very much thankful to Mr. G. Vinay Kumar who helped us in bringing out this present volume.

**—Editors**

# Contents

*Preface*

*List of Contributors*

**SECTION - I**
**CHILD LABOUR AND STREET CHILDREN**

1. **Child Labour: *Issues and Concerns*** 3
   —*T. Rengasamy*
2. **Issues and Concerns of Child Labour and Street Children** 15
   —*K.Nachimuthu*
3. **Problems of Street Children: *Issues and Concerns*** 25
   —*V. Seeni Natarajan*
4. **A Study on Behavioural Changes Among Children's of Gandhigram Creche Project and Children's Club Members Dindigul District** 32
   —*L. Raja*
5. **Problems of Street Children in Africa** 68
   —*Santosh Kumar Mishra*
6. **Child Labour a Predicament of the Country's Prosperity** 100
   —*Goteti Himabindu & N.V.S.Suryanarayana*
7. **Strategy for Eradication and Elimination of Child Labour** 111
   —*Y.Sridevi*

## SECTION - II
## CHILD LABOUR/STREET CHILDREN AND EDUCATION


8. **Problems of Child Labour and Education of Working and Street Children in Chennai** 121
*—G.Sundharavadivel*

9. **Non-Formal Education for Street Children** 133
*—Uma Joshi*

10. **Education and Child Development** 144
*—J.Anuradha*

11. **Promoting Reading Habits Among Rural Children** 150
***Gri Experience in Dindigul District, Tamil Nadu***
*—L.Raja*

12. **Education for 'US'** 164
*—A.Jahitha Begum*

13. **Say No to 'Child Labour' Say Yes to 'Education'** 170
*—Y. Bhaskaracharyulu, Kapu Deepthi & Y. Nirmala*

14. **Teachers' Attitude Towards Inclusion of Children with Hearing Disability** 186
*—P. Renuka & V. Jagadeeswari*


## SECTION - III
## CHILD RIGHTS


15. **Rights of Children: *Issues and Concerns*** 201
*—K. Devan & S. Vidhyanathan*

16. **Awareness of Child Rights** 205
*—R.S.S.Nehru & Y. Bhaskaracharyulu*

17. **Status of Child Rights in India**
***A Critical Appraisal*** 221
*—C. Jim Jesudoss*

18. **Rights of an Indian Child** 230
***With Special Reference to Juveniles***
*—C.Gayatri Devi*

**19. Child Rights and Child Labour in India** 245
*—G. Vidyavathi*

**20. Child is a Blossom but not a Burden** 252
*—B.Praveena Devi*

***Index*** 257

# List of Contributors


1. **Prof. T. Rengasamy**, Professor of Adult Education, Annamalai University, Annamalai Nagar, Tamil Nadu *e-mail:* rengaswamy@yahoo.com
2. **Dr. K.Nachimuthu**, Assistant Professor, Department of Education, Periyar University, Salem District, Tamil Nadu. *e-mail*: drknedn@gmail.com
3. **Prof. V. Seeni Natarajan**, Professor, Department of Life Long Learning, Gandhigram Rural Institute, Gandhigram. *e-mail:* seeninatarajan@yahoo.com
4. **Prof. L. Raja**, Professor, Department of Lifelong Learning & Extension, Gandhigram Rural Institute – Deemed University, Gandhigram – 624 302, Dindigul District, Tamil Nadu & Vice-Presidents of Indian Adult Education Association, New Delhi, *e-mail:* drlingamraja@gmail.com
5. **Dr. Santosh Kumar Mishra**, Technical Assistant, Population Education Resource Centre (PERC), Department of Continuing and Adult Education and Extension Work, S.N.D.T. Women's University, Mumbai - 400 020. *e-mail:* drskmishrain@yahoo.com
6. **Ms. Goteti Himabindu**, Vice-Principal, Sun D.Ed College, Vizianagaram, *e-mail:* gotetihimabindu@yahoo.com
7. **Dr. N.V.S.Suryanarayana**, Teaching Associate, Department of Education, Andhra University campus, Vizianagaram. *e-mail:* suryanarayana_nvs@yahoo.com

9. **Smt. Y.Sridevi**, Teaching Associate, I.A.S.E., Andhra University, Visakhapatnam. *e-mail:* Ysridevi.iase@gmail.com
10. **Dr. G.Sundharavadivel**, Assistant Professor, Department of Adult and Continuing Education, University of Madras, Chennai - 600 005. *e-mail:* drsundara_unom@yahoo.com
11. **Prof. Uma Joshi**, Dean, Faculty of Family and Community Sciences, The Maharaja Sayajirao University of Baroda, Vadodara. *e-mail*: umajoshi554@yahoo.com
12. **Dr. J. Anuradha**, Lecturer in English, Prema College of Education, Thimmapuram, Visakhapatnam *e-mail:* anurahda_jami@yahoo.in
13. **Dr. A.Jahitha Begum,** Associate Professor & Head, Department of Education, Gandhigram Rural University, Dindigul Dt., Tamil Nadu, India. *e-mail:* jahee_j@yahoo.co.in
14. **Prof. Y. Bhaskaracharyulu**, Professor, Department of Education (Merged), Andhra University, Visakhapatnam. *e-mail:* bhaskaryerroju@rediffmail.com
15. **Ms. Kapu Deepthi**, IGNOU, New Delhi. *e-mail*: deepthi.kapu@gmail.com
16. **Dr. (Smt.) Y. Nirmala**, Andhra University, Visakhapatnam.
17. **Dr. P. Renuka**, Assistant Professor, Department of Education S.P. Mahila Visvavidyalayum, Tirupati (AP).
18. **Smt. V. Jagadeeswari**, Academic Consultant, School of Engineering & Technology, SPMVV, Tirupathi & Research Scholar, Department of Adult Education S.V. University Tirupati (AP). *e-mail*: vjadadeeswari@yahoo.co.in
19. **Dr. K. Devan**, Associate Professor, Centre for Adult and Continuing Education, Pondicherry University. *e-mail:* kdevan63@gmail.com
20. **S. Vidhyanathan**, Research Scholar, Centre for Adult and Continuing Education, Pondicherry University. *e-mail:* svidhyanathan@gmail.com

21. **Dr. R.S.S.Nehru**, Reader/Associate Professor, Benniah Christian College of Education, Rajahmundry, AP.
22. **C. Jim Jesudoss**, Research Scholar, Department of Lifelong Learning, Gandigram Rural Institute, Gandhigram.
23. **Dr. C.Gayatri Devi**, Teaching Associate, Dr. B.R.Ambedkar College of Law, Andhra University, Visakhapatnam - 530 003. *e-mail:* gayatridevic@yahoo.co.in
24. **Smt. G. Vidyavathi**, Teaching Associate, I.A.S.E, Andhra University, Visakhapatnam.
    *e-mail:* vidyavathi.g2011@gmail.com
25. **Dr. B. Praveena Devi**, Teaching Associate, Department of Education, AU Campus, Vizianagaram.

# SECTION – I

## CHILD LABOUR AND STREET CHILDREN

## *ISSUES AND CONCERNS*

# Child Labour
## *Issues and Concerns*

– T. Rengasamy

## Introduction

The problem of Child Labour is not a concomitant of modern society only. In fact, the problem has been there since the very dawn of human civilization. The reasons responsible for this phenomenon are varied and have been changing as the years rolled on. Avenues of Child Labour over the years have broadened and so from social forums of public platforms. It has gone into the inner circles of legislative, executive and judicial chambers where its manifestations and remifications are being debated and discussed. The onslaught of industrial and technological revolutions coupled with the changing life styles have added new-dimensions to the whole problem. As a matter of fact the problem is vexed and widespread and is not a characteristic of any particular type of economy. It is prevalent even in advanced countries of the world though in a disguised form. However, the plight of children working in the unorganised sector is more deplorable. The debate on this subject was initiated when government announced its intention in 1985 to introduce fresh legislation to deal with the phenomenon of Child Labour.

## Concept

The term 'child labour' is generally used to refer to, "Any work by children (under 14 years of age, in case of India) that interfere with their full physical and mental development, the opportunities for a desirable minimum of education and of their needed recreation". In reality, children do a variety of works in widely divergent conditions. At one end of the continuum, it is palpably, destructive or exploitative. At the other end, the work may be beneficial, providing or enhancing a child's physical, mental, spiritual, moral or social development without interfering with schooling, recreation and rest. Several attempts made to provide a distinction by differentiating between "Child Work" and "Child Labour". Child work is considered as permissible, while the child labour is prohibitive.

According to the U.N. Convention on the Rights of the Child (Article 32), "State parties recognize the right of the child to be protected from economic exploitation and from performing any work that is likely to be hazardous or to be harmful to the child's education, or to be harmful to the child's health or physical, mental, spiritual, moral and social development." Child Labour therefore is the work, which involves, a degree of exploitation, i.e. physical, mental and economic. It denies the joy to children and access to social opportunities (like education, family love and attention), which eventually impairs the personality and creativity, the evolution and growth of full being and the health, and mental development of a child.

## Definition

UNICEF, determined that child labour is exploitative if it involves.

- Full- time work at too early an age

- Too many hours spent working
- Work that extert undue physical, social or psychological stress
- Work and life on the streets in bad conditions
- Inadequate pay
- Too much responsibility
- Work that hampers access to education
- Work that is determinate to full social and psychological development.

**ILLo's Definition**

Child labour includes children prematurely leading adult lives, working long hours for low wages under conditions damaging to their health and to their physical and mental development, some times separated from their families, frequently deprived of meaningful educational and training opportunities that could open up for them a better future.

Homer Folks, Chairman of United States National Child Labour Committee, defines child labour as "Any work by children that interferes with their full physical development, their opportunities for a desirable minimum of education or their needed recreation."

Another yardstick is to measure child labour is the definition given by Operations Research Group is as follows:

> "A working child as that child who was enumerated during the survey as a child within the 5-15 age bracket and who is at remunerative work may be paid or unpaid and busy any hour of the day within or outside the family."

V.V. Giri has distinguished the term child labour into two senses:

1. Economic practice; and
2. Social evil:
   - Employment of children in gainful occupation with a view to adding to the income of the family.

– The dangers to which the children are exposed i.e. the denial of opportunities of development.

**Reasons for Child Labour**

The following are the reasons for the child labour:

1. Broken families
2. Uncared parents
3. Run Aways
4. Orphans
5. Who work to support parents due to poverty
6. Bounded labour
7. Parents who could not afford to educate their children
8. Following traditional and age- old occupational practices
9. Failure of law and order implementation
10. Illiterate parents who do not educate their children
11. Improper government Policies on education
12. Girl child discrimination
13. Too long distances of schools in rural areas

**Classification of Child Labour**

Child Labour can also be classified as:

**1. Domestic work**

This includes the jobs undertaken by children. For domestic purposes like caring for younger sibling, cooking, cleaning, washing, fetching water, etc. Girls in their families mostly perform these tasks. Although domestic service need not be hazardous, but children in domestic service may well be the most vulnerable and exploited children, as they are most difficult to protect, due to the hidden nature of the work. These children remain away from basic elementary education.

**2. Non-domestic and Non-monetary work**

This is a major form of child activity in subsistence economies, and encompasses farming, hunting, gathering and household/cottage industrial activities. In an agrarian economy like India, children spend a great deal of time in such activities like looking after the cattle, grazing goats, collecting fodder and scaring away birds. They are gradually involved with full-time agricultural work. Naturally such children are deprived of schooling, play and social activity, which impedes their mental development and creativity. Children under the category, whether in agriculture, plantation or in cottage industry are engaged either independently or as part of family labour.

### 3. Bonded Child Labour

Tied or bonded labour is a manifestation of a "Feudal or Semi-Feudal" structure of the society and the economy. Children are bonded both in the agriculture and in the unorganized sector. The principal feature is the pledging of children against a loan (small or large) or an agreement between the child's parents and the employer, whereby, the child would work throughout his or her life or part of life in exchange for money or food. There lifelong service never succeeds even in reducing the debt. Children are lured away or pledged by their parents for parltry sums of money. Most of them are kept in captivity, tortured and made to work 12 to 16 hours a day. The reasons for bondage could be immediate need for money (for purposes like medical treatment, repayment of earlier loan, marriage of daughters, etc) or agreement to replace the bonded worker with a healthier sibling child worker.

### 4. Wage Labour

Wage labour is one of the major types of work activity for children. Wage labour includes work in domestic service, cottage industries, manufacturing processes, industries, and other service activities. They work either as a part of the family labour force or as wage workers. They are often preferred to adults, because of low wages, docile nature and pliability. Wages are paid on a piece rate basis, applying tremendous pressure to work faster.

### 5. Commercial and sexual exploitation of children

Commercial and sexual exploitation, especially for girls is common worldwide. Girls are lured or forced into this form of hazardous labour, which can verge on slavery. The physical and psychological damage inflicted by commercial sexual exploitation makes it one of the most hazardous forms of child labour, These children are not only subjected to risks of HIV/AIDS, sexually transmitted diseases, unwanted pregnancies and drug addiction but are also plunged into a distorted reality where "violence and distrust, shame and rejection are the norms."

### 6. The child combatant

This is another form of child labour exploitation very much discussed currently at the national and international level. This could be the most difficult challenge in the new millennium. There is a need to address the pull and push factors, which facilitate the recruitment of children as combatants. These factors range from education to gainful employment. There is certain amount of self-prestige of being a hero. Even though we rehabilitate child combatants who have surrendered to government forces, when they return to their community they rejoin as combatants, if they fail to secure the promised employment. We have to identify the most appropriate strategies to sustain their withdrawal and to prevent others from joining as combatants. We have to focus on the training of war trauma counsellors to address the psychological impact created in the minds of war combatants. Shelters and other supporting facilities should be in place to accommodate the victims.

**Harmful Effects of Child Labour are:**

1. Future is marred
2. Exposed to more severe risks in unregulated sector of the economy
3. Eye sight damage-working in mines and electric filaments

4. Dangers of pesticides and fertilizers
5. Hazardous occupations – Match Works, Fire Works, Glass and Bangle Manufacture, Diamond Cutting and Polishing, Stone Quarries and Carpet Weaving
6. Radio active waste from hospitals and medicine and leaking bottles
7. Lungs being grossly impaired
8. Deformation in their bodies (Carpet Industries).
9. Mental and Physical retardation
10. Victims of Industrial Accidents
11. Sexual abuse by underworld or thugs
12. Unemployment among adults
13. Technological upgradation

**Implication of in Appropriate Work for Children**

The work by children, purely for profit motive cannot be justified at the cost of the child's health, education and mental, physical and psychological development. The work takes a heavy toll physically, emotionally and intellectually. They are subjected to all kinds of occupational hazards and diseases, as they are frequently more vulnerable because of their growing bodies, their lower threshold for toxics and their lesser ability to respond effectively to hazards. Children are especially vulnerable to accidents because they have neither the awareness of the dangers or knowledge of the precautions to be taken at work. It is often found that children and young workers tend to have more serious accidents than adults. The presence of children in these occupations will affect their life and limbs, their health, their psyche and their total development.

Children working continuously long hours suffer from excessive fatigue and are susceptible to infectious diseases. Stunted growth is common among the working children. The work performed is frequently too demanding in relation to their size and strength, causing irreversible damage to their physical and physiological development, resulting in permanent disabilities, with serious consequences for their adult lives. In some occupations, children are exposed for long hours every day to toxic fumes or industrial waste. Children are particularly sensitive to exposure to solvents, lead, mercury and benzene. These toxic substances are handled by children in leather, construction activity, glass works, repair of automobiles, and mining activities. The effects of repetitive action, postures of sitting, like in the case of carpet weaving can result in muscular-skeletal damage permanently. Carrying heavy loads or being forced to adopt unnatural positions at work can permanently distort or disable growing bodies. Some work situations expose children to unprotected machinery, the risk of explosions and industrial accidents like in case of fireworks, glasswork, etc. The work may damage their eyesight.

A less visible form of exploitation against children is commercial sexual exploitation. It is one of the most brutal forms of violence against children. The child victims suffer extreme physical, psychosocial and emotional abuse, which have life-long threatening consequences. They risk early pregnancy, maternal mortality, sexually transmitted diseases and HIV/AIDS. Sexual exploitation of children has significant emotional ramifications as the victims are unable to return to a normal way of life and are psychologically scared by the experience. In Mumbai, India many young prostitutes were found to have sexually transmitted diseases with a significant, proportion of cases having AIDS. The girls are often victims of beatings, verbal abuse and sexual molestation and rape in the brothels. The inappropriate work and living conditions in the streets of cities harms them indirectly by depriving them of positive experiences of future life. They remain left of education, play and rest, the basic requirements for mental, physical and psychological development. The opportunities lost for learning and growth, reduce their chances of prosperity in life and contributes to the perpetuation of increasing poverty and social underdevelopment from generation to generation.

## Issues of Working Children

The presence of child labour is one of the major concerns facing the international community. There are determined efforts to respond to the issues and at the same time arrive at progressive solutions. The convention on the Rights of the child contains a number of provisions pertaining to children's work, which together provide a framework for policy and action. The convention requires that children by protected from all exploitative and hazardous work, and from work that interferes with their education and full development. To ensure this, the state is required to set minimum ages for employment and regulate working conditions (Article 32). The convention also recognizes the right of children to the means for survival (Article 6). The uncomfortable reality in India is that children's work is often the only apparent avenue to their survival. In the context of widespread poverty and absence of a welfare system that guarantees a livelihood for children and their families, work remains the most viable option for many children. The responses form the state and the society must cover their protection as well as tackle the problems that make their work a necessity. The convention calls to authorities to support parents in their effort to ensure their children's optimal development and adequate standard of living (Articles 18, 27). The convention also guarantess access to free, relevant, high quality education which is a critical element in resolving the issue of child labour. While governments and civil societies progress towards eradicating inappropriate child labour and presence of street children, they must address their concerns and ensure their access to education, a high quality of healthcare, rest and leisure, and acceptable working conditions.

## Problems of Working Children

The impact of work on a child's development is the key to determining when such work becomes a problem. Work that is harmless to adults can be extermely harmful to children. Among the aspects of a child's development that can be endangered by work are:

- Physical development: Including overall health coordination, strength, vision and leaning.
- Cognitive development – Including literacy, numerical and the acquisition of knowledge necessary to normal life.
- Emotional Development: Including adequate self esteem, failing attachment, feelings of love and acceptance.
- Social and moral development : Including a sense of group identify, the ability to co-operate with others and the capacity to distinguish right from wrong.

Education helps a child develop cognitively, emotionally and socially and it is an area often gravely jeopardized by child labour. Work can interfare with education in the following ways:

- It frequently absorbs so much time that school attendance is impossible.
- It often leaves children so exhausted that they lack the energy to attend school or cannot study effectively when in class.
- Some occupations, especially seasonal agricultural work, cause children to miss too many days of class even though they are enroled in school.
- The social environment of work sometimes undermines the value children place on education, something to which street children are particularly vulnerable.
- Children mistreated in the workplace may be so traumatized that they cannot concentrate on school work or are rejected by teachers as disruptive.

**Government Initiatives for the Working Children**

The experts who framed the Indian Constitution consciously in corporated related provision in the constitution. to secure labour protection for children (Articles 24 and 39 (e) and (f) and compulsory universal elementary education (Article 45).

1. National Policy for Children (NPC) in August 1974.

2. The Child Labour (Prohibition and Regulation) Act (CLA), 1986.
3. National Policy of Education (NPE - 1986) and National Policy on Child Labour 1987.
4. The National Child Labour Policy (NCLP) approved in 1987 envisaged a project based Plan of Action to reduce the incidence of Child Labour in the hazardous occupations.

**Conclusion**

Children are not only the budding and blooming flowers of the garden of soceity but also the future backbone of a nation. No more time should be allowed to continue as Child Labour only by.

- When the true conscience of our nation is awakened.
- When all the policy makers and the bureaucrats taken the issue of child labour seriously and commit themselves to the cause of the holistic development of every child in India.
- When the employers would even contemplate the idea to employing a child for any work which might deny the child of a normal childhood.
- When all the parents will become aware of the jeopardy if child labour take upon themselves the duty of caring the physical, social psychological and mental development of the child. We can reduce the problem to greater extent.

## REFERENCES

A Situational Analysis, NIL, NOIDA.

Bequele, A. and W.E. Myers (1985): First Things First. in Child Labour: Eliminating Work Detrimental to Children, UNICEF/ ILO, Geneva, pp. 6-7.

Bequele, A. and W.E. Myers (1995): First Things First in Child Labour: Eliminating Work Detrimental to Children, UNICEF/ ILO, Geneva, pp. 6-7.

Fyfe, Alec (1989): Child Labour, Cambridge Polity Press.

Human Rights Watch/Asia (1998), Police Abuse and Killings of Street Children in India. Human Rights Watch/Children's Rights Project.

ILLo Report (1995), Child Labour, Targeting the Intolerable.

*Ibid*.

Nandna Reddy (1992): Street Children of Bangalore.

# Issues and Concerns of Child Labour and Street Children

– K.Nachimuthu

## Introduction

The problem of child labour exploitation is a major challenge to the progress of developing countries. Children work at the cost of their right to education which leaves them permanently trapped in the poverty cycle, sadly without the education and literacy required for better-paying jobs. Child labour is estimated to be as large as 60 million in India, as many children are "hidden workers" working in homes or in the underground economy. In the long run, this phenomenon will evolve to be both a social and an economic problem as economic disparities widen between the poor and educationally backward states and that of the faster-growing states. Although, the Indian constitution gave a guarantee of free and compulsory education leads to children between the age of 6 to 14, prohibits employment of children.

In some industries children are forced to do repetitive and tedious work like weaving carpets, assembling boxes, polishing shoes, cleaning and arranging shops goods. It is seen that children are found working more in the informal sectors compared to factories and commercial registered organisations. Little children are often seen selling in the streets or working quietly on domestic chores within the high walls of homes- hidden away from the eyes of the media and labour inspectors.

Child labour is a human rights issue of immense sensitivity. Child labour is considered exploitative by the United Nations and International Labour Organisation. The article 32 of the UN speaks about child labour as follows- "States parties recognize the right of the child to be protected from economic exploitation and from performing any work that is likely to be hazardous or to interfere with the child's education, or to be harmful to the child's health or physical, mental, spiritual, moral or social development." To sum up, most countries of the world consider it highly inappropriate when a child below a certain age is put to work.

**Laws about Child Labour**

The first Act to regulate the employment of children and their hours of work was the Factory Act of 1881. A Commission was established in 1929 to fix the minimum age of child employment, on whose recommendation, the Child Labour Act 1933 was passed prohibiting employment of children below 14 yeas of age. The Factories Act of 1948 provided some safeguards to child labourers. In 1986, the Parliament enacted the Child Labour Act (Regulation and Prohibition), planning the employment of children in certain jobs and regulating the condition of work in hazardous occupations. The Juvenile Justice Act came into force on October 2, 1987 after superseding different Children's Act of different States/ UTs.

Based on the recommendations of Gurupadaswamy Committee, the Child Labour (Prohibition and Regulation) Act was enacted in 1986. The Act prohibits employment of children in certain specified hazardous occupations and processes and regulates the working conditions in others. The list of hazardous occupations and processes is progressively being expanded on the recommendation of Child Labour Technical Advisory Committee constituted under the Act and there are a number of loopholes in the act which makes the law ineffective. The Child Labour Act must be non-negotiable and the word "Regulation" should be removed from its title so that child labour abolition becomes non-negotiable. In the same spirit the penal provisions must be enhanced, employment of child labour must be deemed as a cognizable offence and the enforcement machinery strengthened several times over so that the message is clear that child labour will not be tolerated under any circumstances.

India has ratified six ILO conventions relating to child labour and three of them as early as in the first quarter of the 20th century. Through a Notification dated 27 January 1999, the Schedule to the Child Labour (Prohibition and Regulation) Act, 1986, has been substantially enlarged bringing the total number of occupations and processes listed in the Schedule 13 and 51 respectively. The National Policy on Child Labour was formulated in 1987 which enforces legal actions to protect the interests of children, makes development programmes for the benefit of child labour and projects based plan of action in the areas of high concentration of child labour. National Child Labour Projects (NCLP) has been set up to rehabilitate child labour.

Several changes have occurred since the drafting of the National Child Eradication Labour Policy in 1987. A re-examination of all the laws and policies pertaining to working children is critical. There must be consistency in the constitutional and legal provisions pertaining to children's rights especially their right to education and wellbeing. Project based plan of action envisages starting of projects in areas of high concentration of child labour. Pursuant to this, in 1988, the National Child Labour Project (NCLP) was launched in 9 districts of high child labour infelicity in the country. The Scheme envisages running of special schools for child labour withdrawn from work. In the special schools, these children are provided formal/non-formal education along with vocational training, a stipend of Rs.100 per month; supplementary nutrition and regular health check ups so as to prepare them to join regular mainstream schools. The coverage of NCLP scheme has increased from 12 districts in 1988 to 10 districts in the IX plan to 250 districts during the X plan. Under the Scheme, funds are given to the District Collectors for running special schools for child labour. Most of these schools are run by the NGOs in the district.

**Recent Amendments for Child Labour**

As per the 1991 census, the total number of working children in the country was 11.28 million. However, the NSSO survey 1999-2000 has reflected the magnitude of child labour as 10.40 million. It is-proposed to adopt a sequential approach with focus on rehabilitation of children working in hazardous occupations in the first instance. Under the scheme, after a survey of child labour engaged in. hazardous occupations/ processes, the children are to be withdrawn from the above mentioned categories of occupations and processes, and then admitted to special schools (Rehabilitation-cum- Welfare Centres) in order to enable them to be mainstreamed into the formal schooling system. Vocational training is also proposed to be provided under the X Plan strategy. The main objectives are giving stipend, nutrition doubled for special schools, honorarium allotted for health component, budgetary provision for vocational training and training for educational teachers.

Recent amendments carried out include those under the Payment of Wages Act, 1936, the Payment of Bonus Act, 1965, the Apprentices Act, 1961, the Payment of Gratuity Act, 1972, the Employees' State Insurance Act, 1948, the Industrial Disputes Act, 1947, the Plantation Labour Act, 1951, the Maternity Benefit Act, 1961 and the Workmen's Compensation Act, 1923. In addition, the Government introduced in the Parliament Labour Laws (Exemption from Furnishing Returns and Maintaining of Registers by Certain Establishments)

(Amendment) Bill, 2011, the Mines (Amendment) Bill, 2011 and the Inter-State Migrant Workmen (Regulation of Employment and Conditions of Service) (Amendment) Bill, 2011.

The Cabinet Committee on Economic Affairs (CCEA) in their meeting on January 20, 1999 approved continuance of the scheme of National Child Labour Project (NCLP) during the Ninth Plan. The CCEA also approved the increase in the number of such projects from 76 to 100. The Government's commitment to address the problem of child labour is reflected in the statement of National Agenda for Governance (1998), where it says that no child should remain illiterate, hungry/ lack medical care and that measures will be taken to eliminate child labour. (Kacker, 2007).

### Reduction of the Child Labour Wings

On 14.1.2004, 50 new NCLPs were launched in a function held in Vigyan Bhawan. On the basis of census figures of 2001, another new 100 districts have been identified for setting up of NCLPs during the Tenth Plan. As per the census of India 2001, reports that 1,07,53,985 in 1971, 1,36,40,870 child workers in 1981; Child workers of 1,1,2,85,349 persons in 1991 and 1,26,66,377 child workers in 2001. These reports included of the age of five to fourteen age group child workers in India are increased in its stage. On 25$^{th}$ September 2008, The Gazette of India notified that, a list of jobs that covered in different occupations the child workers is banned. As per the data on Child Labour based on Employment Unemployment Survey during NSS 66th Round (2009-10), the survey explains the less amount of child workers comparatively in the old census of 2001. They are; Rural male child workers are 25,11,101 Rural female child workers are 17,27,271; Urban male child workers are 5,46,897 and Urban female child workers are 1,98,602.

### Child Labour in India

India continues to host the largest number of child labourers in the world today. According to the Census 2001, there were 12.7 million economically active children in the age-group of 5-14 years. The number was 11. 3 million during 1991 (Population Census) thus showing an increase in the number of child labourers. Workers in general are classified into main and marginal workers1 by the population census. Census data shows that there is a decline in the absolute number as well the percentage of children (5-14) to total population in that age group, classified as main workers from 4.3 percent in 1991 to 2.3 percent in 2001. But there was a substantial increase in marginal workers in every category of worker irrespective of sex and residence. As a result, despite the number of main workers declining from 9.08 million in 1991 to 5.78 million in 2001, the total number of children in the work force increased. A large part of the increase was accounted for by the increase in marginal workers, which increased from 2.2 million in 1991 to 6.89 million in 2001. The trends between 1991 and 2001 of declining main child workers along with increasing marginal workers may indicate the changing nature of work done by children. This is also to be seen in the context of decelerating employment growth in general in the economy during the last decade.

**Street Children**

The International Day for Street Children was launched on 12th April. It is a new campaign to give a louder voice to the millions of street children around the world so their rights cannot be ignored. The campaign is being supported by Aviva, the world sixth largest insurance group. The International Day aims to give street children a voice and the same opportunities as all children as outlined in the United Nations Convention on the Rights of the Child: the right to protection, participation, provision and prevention from harm. Street children are those who sleep and/or work on the streets, or spend a significant amount of time on the streets. They are some of the most vulnerable and marginalized children in the world, falling through the gaps of state policy and practice. Street children are often invisible and unable to voice their opinions and concerns to those who could make a real difference to their lives. It is up to all of us to help them: together our voices are louder. (Nigam, 1994)

**Laws on Street Children**

In India, 90 per cent of street children are working children with regular family ties who live with their families, but are on the streets due to poverty and their parents' unemployment. The remaining 10 per cent are either working children with few family ties who view the streets as their homes or abandoned and neglected children with no family ties. The National Policy for Children established in 1974 emphasizes the provision of equal opportunities for the development to all children during their growing years. Policy stresses programmes to maintain, educate, and train destitute children and orphans. Policy is also to protect children against neglect, cruelty, and exploitation, but this is only on paper.

An UNICEF study found that almost 40,000 children die every day in developing countries, 25 per cent of whom are in India. Studies in some major cities indicate that the street children in India are of moderate health status, suffering from various chronic diseases and undernourishment. They are deprived of all health programmes, but seem to prefer government hospitals in case of dire need. Street children often have to pay for water. Almost 97 per cent in Calcutta, 99 per cent in Bangalore, and 90 per cent in Madras reported having no access to toilet and bathing facilities; 83 per cent in Kanpur, however, had access to such facilities. Nothing has been heard in recent years of the National Children's Board established in 1975. Apparently the board has gradually waned. Various schemes were planned in 1992 by the Union Welfare Ministry in association with UNICEF. Extending extra health facilities, establishing nutrition programmes, providing vocational training, protecting children from abuse, distributing dry-food poly packs, providing night shelters, providing ration cards, and creating bathing and toilet facilities would go far in improving the quality of life and the future of street children in India.

## Street Children in India

UNICEF's estimate of 11 million street children in India is considered to be a conservative figure. The Indian Embassy has estimated that there are 314,700 street children in metros such as Bombay, Calcutta, Madras, and Kanpur, Bangalore and Hyderabad and around 100,000 in Delhi alone. A survey among 100 street children at the New Delhi Railway Station in India revealed that 86 per cent of boys in the age group 14-18 years were sexually active; however a very low number of them knew about safe sex protection and condom usage. Not one of them reported having ever used a condom.

A study in 2007 in India found the following:

(a) 65.9 per cent of the street children lived with their families on the streets. Out of these children, 51.84 per cent slept on the footpaths, 17.48 per cent slept in night shelters and 30.67 per cent slept in other places including under flyovers and bridges, railway platforms, bus stops, parks, market places.

(b) The overall incidence of physical abuse among street children, either by family members or by others or both, was 66.8 per cent across the states. Out of this, 54.62 per cent were boys and 45.38 per cent were girls.

(c) On a study in India, out of the total number of child respondents reporting being forced to touch private parts of the body, 17.73 per cent were street children. 22.77 per cent reported having been sexually assaulted.

Many of the street children who have run away from home have done so because they were beaten or sexually abused. Tragically, their homelessness can lead to further abuse through exploitative child labour and prostitution. Not only does abuse rob runaway children of their material security, it also leaves them emotionally scarred. Only two in three Indian children have been vaccinated against TB, Diphtheria, Tetanus, Polio and Measles; only one in ten against Hepatitis B. Most street children have not been vaccinated at all. They usually cannot afford, and do not trust, doctors or medicines. (Ray, 2000)

## Department of Education

The department of education has the task of integrating all out of school children which includes child labour and street children into the school system and ensures that children enjoy their right to education. Their function is to prevent children from joining the labour force the education department must ensure that all children in the 5-8 years age group are enrolled and retained in schools; through SSA pay attention to children in the 9-14 age groups like child labour, migrating children, street children, domestic child workers and school dropouts and never enrolled children and provide for residential and non-residential bridge courses, seasonal hostels, mobile schools and work-site schools for children who migrate with their families must from the very beginning be linked to a formal government school.

## Conclusion

In most societies where child labour has been eradicated, multi-pronged strategies were used. Stringent laws were passed which made child labour illegal. In addition the educational system was strengthened so that children removed from work could go to school. Instead of Child labour we can say that, child work'; because children are working in different sectors across the country. The Ministry must strengthen Child line and expanded to every district of the country. A Juvenile Justice Board and a Child Welfare Committee (CWC) must be set up in every district as required in the JJ Act of 2000. There is a need for the Labour department to coordinate its activities with the CWC. The Labour Department should assist children who have completed Class X to get vocational training by linking them up to local ITIs, NGO run vocational training programmes and private sector initiatives. They should not run vocational training centers as the track record of vocational training centers set up by the labour departments is extremely poor.

In general, street children's lives are rather short. They are in bad health, because of their abuse of drugs, venereal disease and Human Immunodeficiency Virus (HIV). Some are killed in conflicts with rival gang groups. Sometimes children's corpses are discovered in the condition in which their internal organs are removed skillfully. They are used for organ transplants in secret. The labour department should instead help older children to get placements in the job market. Youth volunteers, gram panchayats, school teachers, officers of labour department and so on must all be given training about child labour and their respective roles in abolition of child labour. As per 2001 census, the total number of working children between the age group 5-14 years in the country was 1.26 crore. However, as per NSSO survey 2009-10, the working children are estimated at 49.84 lakh which shows declining trend. The reasons giving birth to child labour are poverty, illiteracy, scarcity of schools, ignorance, socially regressive practices, blind customs and traditions, migration and last but not the least corruption amongst employees and government labour organisations. People should not be able to get away with employing and exploiting children.

## REFERENCES

Kacker, L. (2007). Study on Child Abuse: India 2007, Ministry of Women and Child Development, Government of India. pp. 38-39.

Nigam, S. (1994). Street Children of India – a glimpse, Journal of Health Manager, Jan – Jun 1994, Vol. 7., No. 1., pp. 63-67.

Govt. of India (2011). National Child Labour Project, Ministry of Labour and Employment, Govt. of India Publication Retrieved on 2011-09-12.

Ray, Ranjan. (2000). Child Labour, Child Schooling and their Interaction with Adult Labour: Empirical Evidence from Peru and Pakistan'. The World Bank Economic Review, Vol. 14., No 2, pp. 34-67.

UNICEF (2005). Regional Assessment on Violence Against Children in East and the Pacific Region Available at: http:// www.violencestudy.org/IMG /pdf/EAP_2005_Assessment_on_VaC.pdf [Accessed 26 July 2009].

# Problems of Street Children
## *Issues and Concerns*

– V. Seeni Natarajan

**Introduction**

Children are and always shall be a nation's most important resource. One of the most widely accepted truth is that children are the biggest asset. Their contribution is significant for the future well-being of a nation; it is therefore, the primary duty of all countries to give top priority to the welfare of its children. Children constitute the most vulnerable section of the society. Childhood is said to be the foundation laying years in an adult life. Whatever the child experiences through its social contacts, at this stage of life becomes so deeply embedded in the child's mind, that it becomes so difficult to change it or remould it. Children are influenced by the general culture through many channels. Home influences probably outweigh the effects of all other environmental impacts combined in determining the fundamental organisation of the child's behaviour; but, for children who have no homes and who have no parents, to serve as role models, what influences them the most? So it is incumbent upon a nation to make sure that all the children get the optimum conditions for growth enabling thereby survival, developmental, protection and participation. The importance of children in development is unique and complex.

### Child/Juvenile

In 1989, United Nations Convention on the Rights of the Child (UNCRC) defines a child as anyone under the age of 18 years.

According to Juvenile Justice Act – 2000, a juvenile is a child who has not completed the age of 18.

### Who are Street Children?

One of the famous quotation about street children are, "The Street is their home and the pavement is their bed; stray dogs are their friends and the garbage heap is their granary" We can see them all over the city scurrying around like rabbits, rummaging through piles of garbage, cleaning car windows here, trying to sell newspapers, there, polishing shoes, picking rags, carrying luggage etc. They live in a constant fear of police, because they are getting beaten up brutally. They never go to school. They work all days. Since, they have no safe place to keep their earnings, whatever they earn blown-up on movies, drugs, alcohol and other vices. They are the children of the streets. This is the reality for every street child. They are the results of our malfunctioning society and the family within.

Unlike orphans or the handicapped nobody can identify a "Street Child" by any precise scientific criterion. Indeed the expression is hardly a part of the current vocabulary. It covers juvenile delinquents, mal- adjusted children, dropouts and child labour.

UNICEF defines street children as "Those for whom the street more than their family has become their real home, a situation in which there is no protection, supervision or direction from a responsible adult."

## Categories of Street Children

UNICEF classifies defines street children into three categories:

1. Children on the Streets
2. Children of the Streets
3. Abandoned Children.

### 1. Children on the Streets

Children on the streets are those "whose family support base has become increasingly weakened (who) must share in the responsibility for the family survival by working on city, streets and market places. For these children, the home ceases to be the centre for play, culture and daily life. Nevertheless, while the street becomes their daytime activity, most of these children will return home most nights. While their family relationships may be deteriorating, they are still definitely in a place and these children continue to view life from the point of their family."

### 2. Children of the Street

Children of the streets are, "a much smaller number of children who daily struggle for survival without family support, alone on the streets. It is on the streets that they seek shelter, livelihood and companionship. They may maintain occasional contacts with their family.

### 3. Abandoned Children

Abandoned Children are, "those children who have cut off all ties with their families. They live on their own not only for their material survival but also psychologically."

## Issues and Concerns

Street children are subject to malnutrition, hunger, health problems, substance abuse, theft, harassment by the city police and railway authorities, as weli as physical and sexual abuse, neglect, abandonment, child labour, child trafficking, child prostitution, violence and variety of unhealthy family relationships, although the Government of India has taken some corrective measures and declared child labour as illegal.

## Health

Poor health is a chronic problem for street children. Half of all children in India are malnourished, but for street children the proportion is much higher. These children are not only underweight, but their growth has often stunted; for example, it is very common to mistake a 12 year old for an 8 year old. There is much ignorance about reproductive health and many girls suffer needlessly. A girl made infertile by an easily preventable condition may become unfit for marriage and so doomed to a life of even greater insecurity and material hardship. Street children live and work amidst trash, animals and open sewers.

Not only are they exposed and susceptible to disease, they are also unlikely to be vaccinated or receive medical treatment. Only two in three Indian children have been vaccinated against TB, Diphtheria, Tetanus, Polio and Measles and only one in ten against Hepatitis B. Most street children have not been vaccinated at all. They usually cannot afford, and do not trust, doctors or medicines. If they receive any treatment at all it will often be harmful, as with kids whose parents place scalding metal on their bellies as a remedy for persistent stomach pain. Child labourers suffer from exhaustion, injury, exposure to dangerous chemicals, muscle and bone afflictions.

## Poverty

Poverty is the prime cause of the street children crisis. Children from well off families do not need to work, or beg. They live in houses, eat well, go to school and are likely to be healthy and emotionally secure. Poverty dumps a crowd of problems onto a child.

Not only do these problems causing suffering, but they also conspire to keep the child poor throughout his/her life. In order to survive, a poor child in India will probably be forced to sacrifice education and training; without skills the child will, as an adult, remain at the bottom of the economic heap.

## Homelessness

Street children in India may be homeless because their family is homeless through poverty or migration, or because they have been abandoned, orphaned or have run away. It is not unusual to see whole families living on the sidewalks of city roads, or rows of individual children sleeping around railway station. Homeless children have the odds stacked against them. They are exposed to the elements, have an uncertain supply of food, are likely miss out on education and medical treatment and are at high risk of suffering addictions, abuse and illness. A single child alone on the streets is especially vulnerable.

## Child Labour

Child labour is not a new phenomenon. It has existed in one form or the other in all historical periods. What is new, it its perception as a social problem and its being a matter of social concern. In older days the child was viewed with a tender feeling and treated with warmth, mercy, and compassion. But, the fund of knowledge about psycho-physical needs and the environmental influence impinging on his growth and development was rather meager. The mechanics and dynamics of child development were not adequately and scientifically understood.

## Child Prostitution

UN defines child prostitution as 'it is the sexual exploitation of a child for remuneration in cash or in kind usually, but not always, organized by an intermediary.' Child Prostitution, like other forms of child sexual abuse, is not only a cause of death and high morbidity in millions of children, but also a gross violation of their rights and dignity. In the UN report, the investigators estimate the number of children exploited by prostitution is highest in India with estimates between 400,000 and 575,000; Brazil is second with estimates between 100,000 and 500,000; US is the third with 300,000 children and in fourth place is China with 200,000 children. With regard to illness, worldwide, millions of children are infected with sexually transmitted diseases, have abortions, attempt suicide and are raped each year. In parts of Southeast Asia, 50 per cent to 90 per cent of children rescued from brothels are infected with HIV.

**Child Trafficking**

Trafficking is defined as the 'transporting of a person from one place to another through means of deception, kidnapping, actual, threatened or implied violence, and or the abuse individuals actual or perceived by a person in a position of authority e.g. immigration officer, police officer. An individual may trafficked for the purpose of domestic employment, work in the commercial sex industry, manual labour, arranged marriage etc, where people are sold as commodities (i.e. slaves) usually across neighbouring borders, they are often vulnerable as illegal immigrants.

**Child Abuse**

According to WHO, the abuse may be:

1. *Physical abuse:* Physical abuse is the inflicting of physical injury upon a child. This may include burning, hitting, punching, shaking, kicking, beating or otherwise harming a child.
2. *Emotional abuse:* Emotional abuse is also known as verbal abuse, mental abuse and psychological maltreatment. It includes acts or the failures to act by parents, stakeholders that have caused or could cause, serious behavioural, cognitive, emotional or mental trauma.
3. *Neglect:* It is the failure to provide for the child's basic needs. Neglect can be physical, educational, or emotional.
4. *Sexual abuse:* Sexual abuse is inappropriate sexual behaviour with a child. It includes fondling a child's genitals, making the child fondle the adult's genitals, intercourse, incest, rape, sodomy, exhibitionism and sexual exploitation.

Children who are sexually abused are vulnerable to physical, developmental and emotional problems. They are also prone to sexually transmitted diseases including HIV/ AIDS. Sexual abuse and exploitation may lead to use of drugs and alcohol. A child who has been abused has many psychological problems. He or she feels betrayed, worthless, unloved, sad, angry, fearful, isolated, guilty, self-hateful, hostile, distrust others, exhibit tantrums, delayed physical, emotional and mental development, low self esteem etc,. Child Abuse is the ultimate denial of the rights of the child. India has ratified the UN Convention on the Rights of the Child. (UNCRC).

## Conclusion

The street children are trapped in difficult circumstances do not necessarily receive special attention and care. Street children accumulate numerous experiences of violence from an early age and in a range of environments. The street children who have been on the streets are subjected to abuse of all kinds such as physical abuse, emotional abuse, psychological abuse, and neglect. Their risk of exposure to multiple abuses is consistently overlooked in policy development and service delivery for street children.

## REFERENCES

Advanced General Psychology (2002) – A Text Book of Annamalai University.

Child Prostitution – The Ultimate Abuse (1995) – A Report on the National Consultation on Child Prostitution, New Delhi.

Elizabeth B. Hurlock (1996) Developmental Psychology – A Life Span Approach.

Judith Ennew (1994) Street and Working Children – A Guide to Planning, London, Save the Children.

Jim Jesudoss (1994) Street Children: A Problem Associated with Modern Development.

Model Rules under the Juvenile Justice.

United National Convention of the Rights of the Child (2000) – Article 1 p. 63, 197 & 198 (Consideration of Reports Submitted by States Parties, Under Article - 44 of the Convention 2000.

# A Study on Behavioural Changes Among Children's of Gandhigram Creche Project and Children's Club Members Dindigul District

– L. Raja

## Introduction

The children's behaviour at the global level reveals the trends and how it affects them in various stages? Around 40 million children under the age of 14 years are estimated to suffer from abuse and neglect around the world. The world's children are suffering with many problems such as hunger, illness, poverty, malnutrition, anaemia, abuse, sexual abuse, HIV/AIDS, trafficking, violence, child labour and gender discrimination. In the modern era of material and technological advancement, children in almost every country are being callously exploited.

UNICEF, the World's Children's Organisation had issued the statistical data about the children as follows:

- 1 child dying every 4 seconds
- 14 children dying every minute
- Some 92 million children died between 2000 and 2010

- 7.6 million children worldwide died before their $5^{th}$ birthday in 2010
- 1 billion children are deprived of one or more services essential to survival and development.
- 4 million new born worldwide are dying in the first month of life
- 101 million children are not attending primary education, with more girls than boys missing out.
- 2 million children under 15 are living with HIV

Malnutrition is the World's most serious health problem of children which leads to child mortality. The leading causes of child mortality globally are specifically Pneumonia and Diarrhoea. Over 1 million children in Central and West Africa are facing a nutrition crisis.

UNICEF issued a report of The State of World's Children between the year 1980 and 2007. The state of the World's Children has become not only a major reference source of information on children who are being exploited, abused and ignored worldwide, but also offers agenda for their development in education, equality, leadership, participation, health, nutrition and children's rights.

India, the most populous nation in South Asia, has the highest number of age under five deaths in the region and in the world. The prevalence of child abuse is showing an increasing trend in India. In India many children are vulnerable to abuse, exploitation and neglect. Child sexual abuse is a well kept secret in India, and in society there is ignorance, denial and silence about the issue.

With an estimated 12.6 million children engaged in hazardous occupations (2001 Census India), our Country has the largest number of child labourers under the age of 14 in the world. Although poverty is often cited as the cause underlying child labour, there are other factors such as discrimination, social exclusion, as well as the lack of quality education, existing parents' attitudes and perceptions about child labour. In states like Bihar, Mizoram, Rajasthan and Uttar Pradesh, 60 per cent or more girls are dropped out before completing their five years of primary education. Many children in hazardous and dangerous jobs are in danger of injury, and even death.

The nature and scope of trafficking range from industrial and domestic labour, to forced early marriages and commercial sexual exploitation. Existing studies show that over 40 per cent of women sex workers enter into prostitution before the age of 18 years. Moreover, for children who have been trafficked and rescued, opportunities for rehabilitation remains scarce and reintegration process arduous.

The worst sufferer among working children are those who are employed for household work and commonly referred as child domestic workers (CDWs). For a long time the official agencies responsible for protection of children denied their existence. Our constitution prohibits human trafficking and successive governments have formulated laws intended to tackle it, with the primary legislative tool being the Immoral Traffic (Prevention) Act 1956. However these laws are either weak or inadequately enforced.

Children's vulnerability and exposure to violations of their rights remains widespread and multiple in nature. But the real cause of worry is UNIFEM's report which says that 40 per cent of India's police officers are unaware of child trafficking problem.

**Other issues in India**

- Children continue to die of vaccine-preventable diseases such as measles.
- Malnutrition affects nearly half of all children under age five.
- Anaemia affects the vast majority of pregnant women and teenage girls, stunts children's growth and is a leading cause of maternal death and babies with low birth weight.

- Estimates of the number of people in India living with HIV/AIDS range from 2.2 million to 7.6 million. It is estimated that 220,000 children infected by HIV/AIDS and 55,000 to 60,000 children are born every year to mothers who are HIV positive.
- Diarrhoea, often caused by unsafe drinking water or poor sanitation, is the second leading cause of death among children. Access to clean drinking water has improved in recent years, but 122 million households lack toilets.

Society discriminates the female children against their health, education, prosperity and freedom. The problem is worse in conservative Rajasthan than almost anywhere else in India. School enrollment is increasing, but retention and completion rates remain low in part because of the poor quality of the education system, which emphasizes memorization over problem-solving. Women face many forms of gender discrimination. A national preference for male children has led to an increasing gap in gender ratios of children under age six, a trend that may be attributed to female infanticide. It is reported that in Metropolitan cities like Mumbai, Kolkatta, Delhi and Chennai, majority of domestic help are children particularly girls below 14 years.

In India almost 16 per cent of the population comprises of children below six years of age. The prevalence of behaviour problem is socially relevant, and its direction and magnitude will help in understanding child development. In the year 1964, the Department of Adult Continuing Education and Extension now that has been renamed as Department of Lifelong Learning and Extension, Gandhigram Rural Institute, Gandhigram started 13 Balwadies. Later on children's club was started as one of the activities with balwadies. ASMAE India Project came forward to support the children's club activities since 2003. Totally 283 children are members in children's club. The age groups of these children are between 12-18 years studying from 6$^{th}$ to 12$^{th}$ standard. Children's club has been providing a number of activities like skill training, awareness camp and village cleaning activities for all the children.

> "If we are to teach real peace in this world, and if we are to carry on a real war against war, we shall have to begin with the children."
>
> – *Gandhiji*

The Gandhigram crèche project was started in 2005 by Dr. L. Raja, Professor, Department of Lifelong Learning, Gandhigram Rural Institute, Gandhigram with the help of Focolare Movement funding agency, Italy. Initially it was started in a small rented building at Melkaraipudur village of Dindigul District. Then it has been extended and expanded to 14 villages of the neighbouring service villages of GRI. Totally 126 children are under this project. This project has been offering a number of innovative activities such as special skills training in different aspects, educational assistance, educational tour, exposure visits for all children in the project, along with imparting knowledge and creating awareness on environmental protection.

**Background of the Study**

Now-a-days behavioural problems keep on rising among school going children because of family structures, stresses, increasing condition for achievement, small family norms, illness, obesity, malnutrition, sexual violence against children, child trafficking, child labour, child abuse and influence of media etc.

Common behavioural problems in children are psychosocial disorders, habit disorders, Anxiety disorders, Disruptive behaviour, and sleeping problems. Typical problems of school children are aggressive behaviour, memory disorder and learning problems.

In order to overcome from all these problems that the children are facing to-day, Gandhigram crèche project has been providing special skills training in different aspects such as Spoken English, speech skill, Leadership was training,

Vocational training in Computer and Typewriting, Art and handicrafts, Drawing etc. The project has been giving educational assistance for all the children to continue their studies, and also imparting knowledge on health and sanitation and creating awareness on environmental protection. Children's club has been providing a number of activities like skill training on leadership and young facilitators, awareness camp on health and sanitation and village cleaning activities for all the children in the children's club.

There is an urgent need to study the impact of these trainings and to access the behavioural changes of the children in Gandhigram service villages. The Department of Lifelong Learning and Extension has planned a study on "Behavioural changes among children's of Gandhigram Creche Project and children's club members." The purpose of this study is for knowing about the behavioural changes among these children in the aspects of physical, mental, psychological, social, environmental and cultural. This study is not only for identifying the behavioural changes among children, but the opinion and attitudes of the parents and teachers towards their children, and also how the society influences all these factors in the development of children. Though it is a micro study it will serve a ripple effect for the development of the children.

> "Truthfulness, cleanliness, compassion, self-control, magnanimity, contentment, straightforwardness, concen-tration, sense-control, responsibility, equality, tolerance, equanimity and loyalty. And certainly also knowledge, detach-ment, leadership, chivalry, influence, power, dutifulness, independence, dexterity, beauty, serenity and kind-heartedness, as well as ingenuity, gentility, mannerliness, determination, knowledgeability, propriety, pleasantness, joyfulness, immovability, faithfulness, fame and dignity – all these and many others are the everlasting qualities of the Supreme Lord"
>
> – *Srimad Bhagavad Gita" - 1:16*

## Why study children?

There are many reasons to study children's behaviour. Some reasons are scientific while others are practical. From the scientific viewpoint, we study children to increase our knowledge about the ways that development proceeds and the processes that alter their progression. Many behavioural scientists have focused on children's behaviour. Some processes can be observed in simpler form in children than in adults. Others studied children under the assumption that a better understanding of children's behaviour will lead to a better understanding of adult behaviour.

## Methodology

### *Research Design*

The present study was designed to investigate the effect of behavioural changes of the children. 100 students were participated in the present study. Out of these, 50 students were from Gandhigram Creche Project and 50 students were from children's club who are under the Dept. of Lifelong Learning, GRI.

## Objectives

- To study the physical, mental and psychological behaviour of the children.
- To analyze the social interaction, environmental and cultural changes of the children.
- To identify the parents attitude and views on their children's overall development.
- To find out the teachers observation and opinion of the children's educational performance and development.

## Tools Used

Structured Interview Schedule and Questionnaires were prepared and pre-tested to validate the data and make it accurate for good findings.

Sample: There were 3 sections of samples children, teachers and parents.

1. The students studying from $5^{th}$ – $12^{th}$ std the age group was 10-18 years (no=100)
2. Parents of the selected students (n=100)
3. Teachers are undoubtedly the most important components of our educational system.

So school teachers of these selected students were studied (n=100)

**Data Collection**

Both primary and secondary data have been collected for the study.

- Primary data has been collected from the children and from their parents and teachers.
- Secondary data has been collected from the books, journals and internet.

**Area of the Study**

The GCP children were selected from 13 villages of the project service area. Among these villages, the students from Chettiapatty, Oothupatty, Thoppampatty, Amalinagar, Samiyarpatty, Annanagar, and Melkaraipudur villages were studied. Children's club students were studied from 4 villages such as Chettipatty, Ulagampatty, Achampatty and Agaram of Dindigul District.

**Data Analysis**

The statistical data have been analyzed by the techniques of SPSS package and simple tables.

**Major Findings**

It represents the major findings of the study and has been given in three different aspects namely, Children, Parents and Teachers.

**Section – 1: Children**

1. Eighty six per cent of the crèche children were in the age group of 10-14 years and 14 per cent were in 15-18 years. 82 per cent of club children were in the age group

of 10-14 years and 18 per cent in the age group of 15-18 years. With regard to the age groups (10-14) between the crèche children and club children the crèche children's number is more than the club children.

2. Fifty four per cent of the crèche children were female and 46 per cent of crèche children were male. Sixty eight per cent of club children were female and 32 per cent of children were male. With regard to the female percentage between the crèche children and club children the club children's female number is more than the crèche children.
3. Seventy two per cent of crèche children were studying between $5^{th}$-$8^{th}$ standard, 28 per cent of the children studying $9^{th}$-$12^{th}$ standard. Seventy eight per cent of club children were studying between $5^{th}$-$8^{th}$ standard and 22 per cent were studying between $9^{th}$-$12^{th}$ standard. The difference between crèche children and club children studying between $5^{th}$ -$8^{th}$ standard the club children's percentage is higher than the crèche children.
4. Forty eight per cent of crèche children were schedule caste, 28 per cent were from most backward caste and 24 per cent of the children were from backward caste. Half (50%) of the club children were backward caste. 46 per cent were from most backward class and only 4 per cent were schedule caste children. With regard to the schedule caste percentage between the crèche children and club children the club children's number is very less than the crèche children.
5. Ninety six per cent of the crèche children were Hindus and 4 per cent were Christian. 80 per cent of club children were Hindus and 20 per cent were Christian students. With regard to the religion (Christian the minority) percentage between the crèche children and club children the club children's number is higher than the crèche children.
6. Hundred per cent of the crèche children and club children were having good habit of brushing their teeth every day.

7. Thirty six per cent of crèche children developed practice to brush their teeth every day at the age of 5 and 52 per cent of the club children came to understand at the age of 6.
8. Eight six per cent of the crèche children have learned from their mother and 48 per cent of the club children have learned from their father to brush their teeth every day.
9. Sixty per cent of both the crèche children and club children were brushing their teeth one time per day and 40 per cent of both the crèche children and club children were brushing their teeth two times a day. 78 per cent of the crèche children and 66 per cent of the club children were using tooth paste to brush their teeth every day.
10. Hundred per cent of the crèche children and club children were having the practice to wash their face after getting up from the bed, more than one third (36%) of the crèche children came to understand to wash their face at the age of 5 and 6 respectively. And about one third (34%) of the club children came to understand at the age of 6 to wash their face after getting up from the bed.
11. 80 per cent of both the crèche children and club children learned from their mother to wash their face after getting up from the bed.
12. Hundred per cent of the crèche children and club children were washing their face after getting up from the bed.
13. Below half (46%) of the crèche children and club children were washing their face 2 times per day and 4 times per day respectively. Ninety four per cent of crèche children and 92 per cent of club children were using soap to wash their face.
14. Eighty two per cent of the crèche children and about three fourth (76%) of the club children were not having toilet in their house. Only 18 per cent of the crèche children and 24 per cent of the club children were having toilet in their house. Sixteen per cent of the crèche children and 20 per cent of the club children were using

the toilet regularly. Sixteen per cent of the crèche children and 14 per cent of the club children were cleaning their own toilet regularly.

15. 36 per cent of crèche children were using thorn bush and 32 per cent of club children were going near the kanmai (pond) for the toilet, those who were not having own toilet in their house.
16. Ninety eight per cent of both the crèche children and club children were having practice to wash their hand with soap after using the toilet.
17. 32 per cent of the crèche children and 36 per cent of the club children came to understand to wash their hand with soap after using the toilet at the age of 8.
18. Above half (52%) of the crèche children and (42%) of club children came to understand to wash their hand with soap after using the toilet through their teacher.
19. Ninety four per cent of crèche children and 92 per cent of the club children were practicing the habit of washing the hand with soap regularly after using the toilet.
20. Hundred per cent of the crèche children and 98 per cent of the club children were following the habit of washing their hand before eating. It is a good behaviour.
21. Sixty per cent of crèche children and 78 per cent of club children were washing their hand with ordinary water before eating whereas 40 per cent of crèche children and 20 per cent of club children were using soap to wash their hand before eating. The behaviour of washing their hand with soap water has to be insisted from the childhood to avoid the diseases in the future.
22. About three fourth (76%) of the crèche children and most of the (80%) club children were having own bathroom in their house. All the (100%) crèche children and club children were taking bath daily.
23. Regarding the place of taking bath those who were not having own bathroom in their house, 12 per cent of the

crèche children and 18 per cent of the club children were taking bath in open place. 96 per cent of the crèche children and 98 per cent of the club children were taking bath on their own.

24. Eighty six per cent of the crèche children and club children were eating with their parents. 96 per cent of the crèche children and all (100%) the club children were taking food by sitting on the floor.
25. Seventy per cent of the crèche children and 78 per cent of the club children were taking vegetables regularly. Fifty eight per cent of the crèche children and 62 per cent of the club children were not wasting the vegetables. Twenty four per cent of the crèche children were wasting the vegetables rarely and 24 per cent of club children were wasting the vegetables frequently.
26. Ninety eight per cent of the crèche children and club children were going to school regularly. Two third (66%) of the crèche children and 60 per cent of the club children were going to school by walk.
27. Sixty per cent of the crèche children's school time is 8.30 and 36 per cent of club children's school time is 8.30 am. Half of the (50%) crèche children were reaching their school at 8.45 am and 52 per cent of the club children were reaching their school at 8.00 am.
28. Ninety eight per cent crèche children and most of the (92%) club children were attending prayer regularly. 78 per cent of the crèche children and 86 per cent of the club children were just attending the prayer. Ten per cent of crèche children and 4 per cent of club children were singing a song. And 8 per cent of crèche children and 2 per cent club children were organizing prayer in their school.
29. More than one third (36%) of the crèche children were attending prayer regularly for more than 5 years and 30 per cent of the club children were attending prayer regularly since 3 years.

30. Sixty per cent of the crèche children and 44 per cent of the club children were sharing their opinion with the teacher. Twenty four per cent of the crèche children and 32 per cent of club children shared about the subjects. And 36 per cent of crèche children and 12 per cent of club children shared about the general topics.
31. Half of the (50%) crèche children and 40 per cent of the club children shared their opinion with the teacher if they had any doubts. Fourty per cent of the crèche children and 28 per cent of the club children were encouraged by their teacher to share their opinion with the teacher.
32. Regarding the reason for not sharing the opinion with the teacher, 18 per cent of the crèche children were afraid and 36 per cent of the club children hesitated in sharing their opinion.
33. Ninety eight per cent of the crèche children and 96 per cent of the club children were sharing the things with their friends. 50 per cent of crèche children and 16 per cent of club children were sharing study materials & eatables with their friends. And 6 per cent of crèche children and 28 per cent of club children were sharing play materials with their friends.
34. Sixty eight per cent of the crèche children and 58 per cent of the club children were not attending private tuition. Thirty two per cent of the crèche children and 42 per cent of the club children were studying all subjects in the private tuition. Twenty per cent of the crèche children and 34 per cent of the club children were spending 2 hours in the tuition for studying.
35. Ninety two per cent of the crèche children and 94 per cent of the club children were having interest to go for tuition. It shows that what they are getting from the school is not sufficient enough and also many teachers encourage the children to come for tuition so that the teachers earn good money. On the whole the behaviour

of the children to go for tuition clear that they wanted to get good marks too.

36. Forty four per cent of the crèche children have scored $10^{th}$ to $20^{th}$ rank and 42 per cent of the club children have scored 1st to $10^{th}$ rank in their recent exam.
37. Twenty six per cent of the crèche children and 34 per cent of the club children have scored good marks because of tuition. 6 per cent of the crèche children and 20 per cent of the club children have scored good marks in all subjects.
38. Regarding the help/advice given to the children to go for tuition, 20 per cent of crèche children and 22 per cent of club children have got help/advice from their mother.
39. Forty per cent of the crèche children and 38 per cent of the club children were playing both in the play period and after the school hours. Twenty per cent of the crèche children and 30 per cent of the club children were playing after the school hours. It is good that play is very important for the children for physical development.
40. Forty per cent of the crèche children and 48 per cent of the club children were playing in the school ground. 26 per cent of the crèche children and 32 per cent of the club children were playing near the house. Seventy two per cent crèche children and (64%) of the club children were playing with their friends.
41. Nearly one third (32%) of the crèche children and half of the (50%) club children were playing kho-kho. Twenty two per cent of the crèche children and 24 per cent of the club children were playing kabadi.
42. Seventy six per cent of the crèche children and 74 per cent of club children have received help to get more interest in playing; 46 per cent of crèche children have got help from their friends and 30 per cent of club children have got help from their mother to get interest in playing.
43. Hundred per cent of the crèche children and club children love their parents. Most of the (90%) crèche children

and most of the (88%) club children love their parents from childhood. Forty six per cent of the crèche children got advice from their mother to love their parents and 46 per cent of club children got advice from their father. The strong relation with children and parents are clear that the love and affection create good confidence in children.

44. Ninety six per cent of the crèche children and Ninety two per cent of the club children obey their parents and grandparents. crèche children (76%) and club children(72%) obey their parents/grandparents from childhood. Below half (48%) of the crèche children and most of the (68%) of club children have received advice from their mother to obey their parents/grandparents.
45. Ninety four per cent of the crèche children and 88 per cent of the club children were helping their parents in household activities. Sixty per cent of the crèche children and 56 per cent of the club children were doing household activities daily in the morning and evening.
46. Half of the (50%) crèche children and 30 per cent of the club children were helping their parents since 2 years. Thirty per cent of the crèche children and 40 per cent of club children were helping their parents since the age of 7. Sixty two per cent of the crèche children and 58 per cent of club children have got advice from their mother for doing household activities.
47. Eighty two per cent of the crèche children and 86 per cent of the club children were beaten by their parents. Half of the (50%) crèche children and more than half (56%) of the club children were beaten by the parents from their childhood itself. So parents beating their children not make them afraid but disciplined them.
48. Forty per cent of the crèche children and 36 per cent of the club children were beaten for doing mischief. Eighteen per cent of crèche children and 16 per cent of club children were beaten for not studying well/not

getting good marks. According to the reason for not being beaten by the parents. 10 per cent of the crèche children and 8 per cent of club children were not doing any mischief.

49. Ninety per cent of the crèche children and 84 per cent of the club children like their brother/sister. Regarding the specific reason that the children like their brother/sister, above half (52%) of the crèche children and about one third (34%) of the club children were very much attached. And 18 per cent of crèche children and 22 per cent of club children's brother/sister helped in their studies.

50. Two third (66%) of the crèche children and above half (52%) of the club children were liking their brother/sister from the childhood. This kind of kinship is very rare when there is a single child family. The daughter of single (nuclear) family becoming more and more due to various reasons to live separate lifestyle leads to less participation in community life and rarely mingle with others in cities. But the village life style is ok to some extent.

51. Eighty six per cent of the crèche children and 80 per cent of the club children were giving play things to their brother/sister. Below half (46%) of crèche children and above half (52%) of the club children were giving their play things to their brother/sister from the childhood itself. 56 per cent of crèche children and 52 per cent of club children have got advice from their mother to share the play things with their brother/sister.

52. Ninety two per cent of the crèche children and 90 per cent of the club children were scolded by their parents. Thirty four per cent of the crèche children and 24 per cent of club children were scolded for doing mischief. Fourteen per cent of crèche children and 26 per cent of club children were scolded for not studying well/not getting good marks.

53. Sixty two per cent of the crèche children and 70 per cent of the club children do not get scolding from their parents. About one fourth (24%) of the crèche children and above half (52%) of the club children were crying that they don't like scolding from their parents.
54. Thirty eight per cent of crèche children and above half of the (54%) club children have got from 1st to 10th rank, 38 per cent of crèche children and 30 per cent of club children have got from 10th to 20th rank.
55. Forty six per cent of the crèche children and 34 per cent of the club children were having competitive spirit if their friends were getting good marks, and they developed competitive spirit after entering high school. 6 per cent of the crèche children were jealous as well as anger. 10 per cent of the club children were having anger and 2 per cent were jealous. Regarding the children to overcome the bad feelings of anger and jealous, 8 per cent of crèche children and 10 per cent of club children were overcome by the teacher.
56. Regarding the reason for not getting good marks in the exam, 40 per cent of the crèche children and 56 per cent of the club children have not studied well. Thirty six per cent of crèche children and 14 per cent of club children were having exam fear. The exam fear among the children should be taken care by the teacher, parents and society as well.
57. 36 per cent of both crèche children and club children were not getting good marks since 1 year. And 42 per cent of crèche children and 24 per cent of club children were not getting good marks since 2 years.
58. Regarding the help that was given to the children to overcome in not getting good marks, 60 per cent of crèche children and 62 per cent of club children did not answer. Twenty six per cent of crèche children and 24 per cent of club children were able to overcome by their teacher.
59. Eighty four per cent of the crèche children and 94 per cent of the club children were crying. Thirty per cent of

the crèche children and 52 per cent of the club children are crying from childhood.

60. Sixty per cent of crèche children and two third (66%) of the club children cried for being scolded/beaten by their parents.
61. Sixty per cent of the crèche children and 62 per cent of the club children were fighting with their friends. Eighteen per cent of the crèche children fought with their friends within a week and 24 per cent of club children fought with their friends within a month. Twenty six per cent of crèche children and 28 per cent of club children were fighting because of their friends scolding.
62. Seventy per cent of the crèche children and 76 per cent of the club children were having friends in school. Sixteen per cent of both crèche children and club children were having friends in their village.
63. Forty two per cent of crèche children and 40 per cent of the club children were playing and studying with their friends in school. Twenty per cent of crèche children and 18 per cent of club children were playing with their friends in school.
64. Twenty two per cent of crèche children and 20 per cent of club children were playing with their friends in the village. Six per cent of the crèche children and 4 per cent of the club children were playing and doing some creative works with their friends in their village.
65. Eighty eight per cent of the crèche children and 82 per cent of the club children liked to help the poor children. 34 per cent of crèche children and 20 per cent of club children liked to give guidance regarding studies. Thirty per cent of crèche children and 44 per cent of club children liked to give money to the poor children for help them to study without having any break.
66. Thirty per cent of the crèche children and 38 per cent of club children have got advice from their teacher in helping the poor children. Twenty six per cent of the crèche

children have got advice from the Gandhigram Crèche Project training and only 2 per cent of club children got advice from the Gandhigram Children's club.

67. Hundred per cent of the crèche children and 96 per cent of the club children were going to their relatives/friends house. Seventy eight per cent of the crèche children and 72 per cent of the club children were talking with their relatives those who came to their house. Sixteen per cent of crèche children and 14 per cent of club children were talking and playing with their relatives.

68. Ninety six per cent of the crèche children and 80 per cent of the club children have helped the aged and sick people in their village. 34 per cent of crèche children and 44 per cent of club children helped to get medicines/things. 22 per cent of crèche children and 20 per cent of club children helped to carry water for the aged and sick people in their village.

69. Forty four per cent of crèche children and 26 per cent of club children were helping the aged and sick people at their age of 10. Thirty six per cent of crèche children and 40 per cent of club children above ten years were helping the aged and sick people in their village.

70. Thirty eight per cent of crèche children and 28 per cent of club children were advised by their mother to help the aged and sick people. Twenty six per cent of the crèche children were advised by their mother & GCP training and 8 per cent of club children were advised by their mother & GRI children's club training.

71. Eighty eight per cent of the crèche children and 92 per cent of the club children have planted saplings. Below half of the (46%) crèche children and above half of the club children (56%) have planted from 1 to 3 saplings. 20 per cent of crèche children and 10 per cent of club children have planted more than 6 saplings.

72. Forty two per cent of the crèche children's saplings and more than half (54%) of the club children saplings grown

below 2 numbers. Below half (46%) of the crèche children and above half (52%) of club children have planted the saplings before 1 year.

73. Below half (48%) of the crèche children have got advice from Gandhigram crèche project training to plant the saplings. Only 8 per cent of club children have received advice from their mother and children's club children have received advice from their mother and children's club. 10 per cent of crèche children and more than one third (38%) of the club children have received advice from their mother to plant the saplings.

74. Regarding the children's alertness if water is flowing from the public tap in their village, most of the (60%) crèche children and 48 per cent of the children stated that they were try to stop. And 40 per cent of the crèche children and 44 per cent of the club children stated that they asked others to stop.

75. Forty per cent of the crèche children and 58 per cent of the club children have participated in village cleaning activities. 24 per cent of crèche children and 26 per cent of club children have been participating in village cleaning activities once in a year.

76. Twenty four per cent of crèche children and 26 per cent of club children have started to participate in village cleaning activities since 1 year.

77. Fourteen per cent of the crèche children have received advice from their teacher and about one third (34%) of the club children have received advice from balwadi teacher/children's club to participate in village cleaning activities.

78. Regarding the children being a member in social activities in their school, 60 per cent of crèche children and 28 per cent of club children were not taking part in any activities. Twenty two per cent of the crèche children were taking part in Junior Red Cross and below half (44%) of the club children were taking part in Green Revolution.

79. Seventy eight%) of the crèche children and 82 per cent of the club children have gained knowledge about the environmental problems. Twenty six per cent of the crèche children came to understand regarding environmental problems from 6th std onwards and 28 per cent of club children came to understand from 5th onwards.
80. Fifty two per cent of the crèche children and 60 per cent of the club children understood the environmental problem by the teacher, 12 per cent of crèche children understood after GCP training and 14 per cent of the club children understood the environmental problem by the children club activities.
81. Below half (48%) of crèche children and 50 per cent of the club children have approached to reduce the noise pollution in their village at the time of exam.
82. hirty four per cent of crèche children and 26 per cent of club children have approached since in 1 year to reduce the noise pollution in their village. 24 per cent of crèche children and 36 per cent of club children received advice from their teacher in approaching to reduce the noise pollution at the time of exam.
83. Seventy two per cent of the crèche children and 90 per cent of the club children participated in cultural programme in their school or in village. Above one third (36%) of the crèche children and below half of the (44%) club children have participated in dance.
84. Above one third (36%) of the crèche children and below half (48%) of the club children have participated from above 6th standard onwards. Forty per cent of the crèche children and more than half (56%) of the club children were encouraged by their teacher to participate in cultural progamme in school/village.
85. Ninety eight per cent of the crèche children and 86 per cent of the club children liked to participate in cultural programme. Twenty per cent of crèche children liked to participate in all programmes and 32 per cent of club children liked to participate in dance.

86. Thirty per cent of the crèche children got interest to participate in cultural programme from childhood and 28 per cent of the club children have interest from 6$^{th}$ standard onwards.
87. Ninety six per cent of the crèche children and Ninety four per cent of the club children were encouraged by their parents to participate in cultural programme. 30 per cent of crèche children and 20 per cent of club children were encouraged by their parents to participate in all programme.
88. Thirty eight per cent of the crèche children and Forty per cent of the club children were encouraged by their parents to participate in cultural programme from 6$^{th}$ standard onwards. Two third (66%) of the crèche children and below half (48%) of the club children's parents got inspiration in encouraging their children to participate in cultural programme by observing other children's participation in cultural programmes.
89. Sixty per cent of the crèche children and 56 per cent of the club children participated in religious activities in the family/village, 54 per cent of crèche children and 56 per cent of club children participated in religious activities during the festival time.
90. Twenty per cent of the crèche children participated since 3 years and 18 per cent of the club children participated since 2 years in the religious activities. Forty per cent of the crèche children and 52 per cent of the club children were motivated by their mother to participate in religious activities in their family/village.
91. Crèche children are more vulnerable group (schedule caste) they come from the backward village and very poor family background and uneducated. They are also malnourished and very slow in learning and the competitive spirit is very low in nature due to the surroundings in which they come from unable to cope with the other children in the school and in the village. Therefore, their performance level is slow when compare to club children.

**Section – 2: Parents**

1. Ninety eight per cent of the crèche children's parents observed the personal cleanliness behaviour of their children and 100 per cent of the club children's parents have observed the personal cleanliness behaviour of their children.
2. Eighty six per cent of the crèche children's parents and about three fourth (76%) of the club children's parents stated that their children were having the cleaning behaviour.
3. 40 per cent of the crèche children were practicing the cleaning activities at the age of 5 and 48 per cent of club children were practicing the cleaning activities above the age of 5.
4. Ninety two per cent of the crèche children and 88 per cent of club children were guided by their mother to practice personal cleanliness.
5. Ninety eight per cent of the crèche children and club children's parents stated that their children were following the cleaning activities regularly in the morning.
6. The crèche children (74%) and club children (86%) were taking part in extracurricular activities.
7. Thirty eight per cent of crèche children have taken part in dance whereas 32 per cent of club children have taken part in computer training as extracurricular activities.
8. Nearly one third (32%) of the crèche children and about one fourth (26%) of the club children were taking part in extracurricular activities at the age of 8.
9. Thirty four per cent of crèche children were motivated by their mother and 42 per cent of club children were motivated by their teacher to take part in sports/games and extracurricular activities.
10. Fourteen per cent of crèche children and 10 per cent of club children were not interested and involved to take part in extracurricular activities.

11. Regarding the health condition of the children for the past 5 years, above half (54%) of the crèche children and 64 per cent of the club children were healthy.
12. Hundred per cent of crèche children have received money from Gandhigram crèche project but club children's parents have not received any money from children's club.
13. 84 per cent of crèche children parents have got money only from Gandhigram Crèche Project (GCP) and 16 per cent of them have got money from both GCP and from outsiders. And Sixteen per cent of club children's parents borrowed money from others for their children's health improvement.
14. The crèche children (76%) and most of the club children (88%) were taking food properly from the childhood.
15. Seventy per cent of the crèche children and 64 per cent of the club children were having the habits of not wasting the food.
16. Sixteen per cent of crèche student's parent and 18 per cent of club children's parents scolded their children for wasting food.
17. In doing different household activities regularly by the children, 16 per cent of crèche children were doing the work of carrying water and sweeping house and 26 per cent of club children were doing the work of carrying water and going to shop.
18. Ninety six per cent of the crèche children and 90 per cent of the club children were having the habits of attending school regularly.
19. Two per cent of the crèche children and 6 per cent of club children were in poor health condition; therefore they could not attend school regularly.
20. Below half(48%) of both crèche children and club children were spending 2 hours for study at home, 30 per cent of crèche children and 26 per cent of club children were spending one hour for studying at evening time. 6 per

cent of crèche children and 8 per cent of club children were not studying but always watching TV.

21. Seventy eight per cent of the crèche children and 90 per cent of the club children's parents stated that these children were not hiding any matters from them.
22. Eight per cent of the crèche children were hiding regarding studies and 4 per cent of club children were hiding regarding homework.
23. Twenty per cent crèche children and 40 per cent of club children were obedient/honest to their parents.
24. Sixty per cent of crèche children and 56 per cent of club children's parents do not have the habits of helping their children in studies.
25. Eighteen per cent of the crèche children's parents and 34 per cent of club children's parents were just sitting near their children while studying.
26. Below half (44%) of the crèche children and about one third (34 percent of the club children's parents were uneducated for not helping in studies of their children.
27. Ninety eight per cent of the crèche children's parents and 94 per cent of the club children's parents have visited the school and met the teacher of their children.
28. Almost all of the (96%) crèche children's parents and most of the (84%) club children's parents stated that they have visited the school for their children's improvement.
29. Sixty per cent of crèche children's parents and 62 per cent of club children's parents have visited the school at the time of parents meet. 34 per cent of crèche children and 18 per cent of club children's parents have visited the school once in 3 months.
30. Ninety six per cent of the crèche children and 84 per cent of the club children's parents stated that they were sharing their child's progress with the teacher.
31. Sixty two per cent of the crèche children's parents and 40 per cent of club children's parents have shared regarding their children are studying habits with the teacher.

32. Fifty two per cent of crèche children's parents sharing their children's progress/growth with the teacher once in 3 months and 44 per cent of club children's parents sharing their children progress/growth at the time of parents meet.
33. Sixty six per cent of the crèche children's parents and 74 per cent of the club children's parents stated that the teacher not made any complaints about their children.
34. Regarding the complaints about the children by the teachers, 18 per cent of both the crèche children and club children were not studying well.
35. Eighty two per cent of the crèche children and 74 per cent of the club children's parents stated that their children not having any misbehaviour at home or school.
36. Regarding the misbehaviour among the children, 8 per cent of crèche children's parents said that their children were doing misbehaviour while playing with friends and 12 per cent of club children's parents stated that their children were telling lies regarding studies.
37. Eighty two per cent of the crèche children and 92 per cent of the club children's parents stated that their children were obeying elder member in the family.
38. Sixty four per cent of the crèche children and 58 per cent of the club children were obeying the words of elder members in the family.
39. Regarding the reason for not obeying the elder members, 12 per cent of crèche children and 6 per cent of club children were mischievous.
40. Ninety per cent of the crèche children and 68 per cent of the club children's parents stated that their children were having the habits of sharing all the outside activities with them.
41. Ninety two per cent of the crèche children and 82 per cent of the club children's parents stated that their children were showing anger behaviour.

42. Regarding the reason for getting anger, 28 per cent crèche children and 36 per cent of club children were getting anger for asking to do household work.
43. Fifty two per cent of the crèche children and 50 per cent of the club children were getting anger very rarely.
44. Regarding showing anger towards their parents and othes, 28 per cent of the crèche children and 30 per cent of club children's parents stated that their children do not take food.
45. Fifty eight per cent of crèche children and 44 per cent of club children's parents stated that their children's behaviour of anger had decreased. 36 per cent of crèche children and 38 per cent of club children's behaviour of anger had increased.
46. Regarding the decrease of anger, 30 per cent of crèche children and 22 per cent of club children's behaviour of anger decreased after entering into high school.
47. Regarding the increase of anger, 24 per cent of crèche children and 26 per cent of club children's behaviour of anger increased since 1 year.
48. About one third (32%) of the crèche children's parents said that they beat their children when they get anger and nearly one third (32%) of the club children's parents said that they scold their children when they got anger.
49. Regarding spending their free time, below one third (30%) of the crèche children were playing and 44 per cent of club children were watching TV in their free time.
50. Ninety six per cent of the crèche children's parents and 86 per cent of the club children's parents stated that there was no such problem in spending free time of the children.
51. Regarding the opinion about the skill training that was provided to the children, 56 per cent of crèche children's parents stated that it helped a lot and 72 per cent of club children's parents stated that the skill training was good for their children and this behaviour has changed gradually.

52. Regarding the active participation in children's club activities, all the crèche children were not in children club. 86 per cent of the club children were actively participating in children's club activities.
53. About one fourth (26%) of the club children participated in village cleaning activities and awareness programme. 38 per cent of the club children were actively participating in children's club activities since 1 year and 56 per cent of the children were encouraged by balwadi teacher to actively participate in village cleaning activities. So their behaviour level is better in such activities.
54. Regarding the participation in different activities, 38 per cent of crèche children participated in skill training and tour whereas 24 per cent of club children were participated in religious function, skill training and village cleaning activities.

**Section – 3: Teachers**

1. Seventy eight per cent of the club children were participated in extracurricular activities than the crèche children (58%).
2. Crèche children (32%) participated in games more than the club children (28%).
3. Above one fourth (28%) of the crèche children participated since 1 year and nearly one third (32%) of the club children participated since 3 years in extracurricular activities.
4. Motivation were given to the children to participate in extracurricular activities, above half (52%) of the crèche children and more than half (58%) of the club children were motivated by the teachers.
5. Eighty per cent of the crèche children and 88 per cent of the club children were attentive in their class room.
6. Most of the (60%) crèche children and nearly three fourth (74%) of the club children were motivated by their teachers to be attentive in the classroom.

7. Below half (44%) of the crèche children and nearly more than half (52 percent of the club children were good in their studies.
8. More than half (58 percent of the crèche children and 64 per cent of the club children were motivated by the teachers for being good in studies.
9. Both the crèche children and club children (18%) had improved in discipline. Crèche children (12%) improved in studies than the club children (4%).
10. Club children have got from 1st to 5th rank more than the crèche children in both quarterly and half yearly examination.
11. Crèche children (56%) studied well than the club children (52%) in last academic year.
12. Eighty per cent of the crèche children and 84 per cent of the club children answered the questions to the teacher.
13. Forty six per cent of the crèche children and 30 per cent of the club children provided answer in one word orally, and 18 per cent of the crèche children and 26 per cent of the club children provided answer in sentence for the questions to the teacher.
14. Sixty eight per cent of the crèche children and 76 per cent of the club children were motivated for answering the questions by the teachers.
15. Seventy eight per cent of the crèche children and 80 per cent of the club children do not hide anything from the teacher.
16. Crèche children (40%) were obedient compared to the club children (28%) and they did not hide anything from the teacher.
17. Club children (48%) understood fully than the crèche children (36%) that were taught by the teacher.
18. Fifty six per cent of the crèche children and 52 per cent of the club children have understood the subjects from 5th std onwards.

19.. Seventy six per cent of crèche children and 86 per cent of club children were motivated by their teachers to understand the subject that was taught in the classroom. 14 per cent of crèche children were motivated by Gandhigram Crèche Project whereas only 4 per cent were motivated by Gandhigram children's club.

20. Crèche children (58%) were obedient than the club children (46%) with the teacher in the classroom.

21. Eighty two per cent of the crèche children and 72 per cent of the club children did not share their feelings with the teacher. Club children (28%) shared their feelings more than the crèche children (18%) with the teacher.

22. Forty eight per cent crèche children and 44 per cent of club children hesitated for not sharing their feelings with the teacher.

23. Eighty six per cent of the crèche children and 72 per cent of the club children did not share their personal problems with the teacher. Club children (28%) shared their personal problems more than the crèche children (14%) with the teacher.

24. Ten per cent of crèche children and 22 per cent of club children were motivated by their teachers to share their personal problems.

25. Three fourth (76%) of the crèche children and most of the (80%) club children talked about the current affairs with the teacher. 66 per cent of the crèche children and 74 per cent of the club children were talked about the news with the teacher.

26. Fifty eight per cent of the crèche children and 72 per cent of the club children helped their classmates in studies/writings. Above 38 per cent of the crèche children and 42 per cent of the club children helped their classmates in group study. 30 per cent of both the crèche children and club children helped their classmates in studies since 1 year.

27. Forty six per cent of the crèche children were motivated by their teachers and 34 per cent of the club children were motivated by their parents to help in studies/ writing for their classmates.
28. Ninety per cent of the crèche children and 98 per cent of the club children mixed with their peer group. More than one third (38%) of the crèche children and above half (54%) of the club children were playing and studying with their peer group.
29. Forty per cent of the crèche children and below half (46%) of the club children mingled with their peer group since 2 years.
30. Thirty six per cent of the crèche children and 48 per cent of the club children mixed with their peer group for the purpose of games and group study.
31. Sixty per cent of the crèche children and 54 per cent of the club children did not get anger and fight with their friends.
32. Club children (34%) have got anger and fought with their friends more than crèche children (28%).
33. Twenty percent of the crèche children and 26 per cent of the club children got anger with their friends since 1 year.
34. Club children (56%) participated more than the crèche children (32%) in cultural programmes.
35. Twenty four per cent of the crèche children and 50 per cent of the club children were participated in group event in the cultural programme.
36. Twelve per cent of crèche children and 32 per cent of club children participated in the cultural programme since 1 year.
37. Sixty per cent of the crèche children and 50 per cent of the club children's teachers stated that the skill training was useful for the students.
38. Fifty four per cent crèche children were benefitted after Gandhigram Crèche project skill training programme and

44 per cent of the club children were benefitted after joining in children's club of Gandhigram.

39. Regarding the suggestion for further improvement in extracurricular activities, teachers stated that the training should be given in studies for 52 per cent of crèche children and for 46 per cent of the club children than any other extra-curricular activities. 18 per cent crèche children's teacher has pointed out for computer training and 12 per cent for spoken English classes. 22 per cent of club children teacher stated about the computer training and 20 per cent for spoken English classes.

40. Regarding the vocational skill development for the children, 20 per cent of crèche children's teachers and 12 per cent of club children's teachers suggested for tailoring classes.

41. Regarding the value based education for the children, 18 per cent of crèche children's teachers suggested for adolescent behaviour and 30 per cent of the club children's teachers suggested to educate adolescent problem and behaviour.

**Suggestions**

- Close cooperation between teachers, parents, and health care providers are necessary to ensure healthy development of the children.
- Attitudes towards children should be changed significantly to improve their education.
- The school should pay very close attention to the development of the parental education. The relationship between the parents and schools should be in co-operation.
- Should create awareness for both (the children and the parents) on how to overcome their problems?
- Anti child labour laws should be enforced by the Government.

- Education and health are important parameters for children's development. Government and Non-governmental organisations should provide services to the children and families to survive and protect them from crisis such as poverty, malnutrition and infectious disease.
- Because of malnutrition regular clinical test by Government physicians in all schools may help to prevent the health problem.
- Periodic de-worming, anti-anemia measures, nutrition education and hygiene education should be provided to the children.
- Children should be encouraged to join the vocational training centers to enhance their skills.
- Training should be provided for the children to improve their academic performance.
- Teachers and Parents are suggested for improving their awareness on adolescent health and adolescent problems.
- Counselling should be provided for the problematic children by the Government schools.
- Government should impart an orientation programmes for the teachers on learning behavioural problems of the children, so that they can identify the problematic children and give them proper training.
- Government should design an effective training system for the teachers by using the advanced techniques like animation and documentary films to educate the children.
- Parent's ability should be improved by giving awareness camp to manage their children's behaviour.
- Environmental education for children is critically important and should start before school begins. Early environmental education experiences help shape children's values, perspectives, and understanding of the environment and how to interact with it?

➢ Children's behaviour can be modified by providing appropriate environmental interventions at various stages.

## Conclusion

Every child is unique in their own way and many qualities have been imbibed by the brought up of their parents, teachers and society. As children grow according to the situation children may exhibit their behaviours either at home or at school. In such a way the behavioural pattern is changing from time to time at various stages.

This study brought out the children's physical development and the personal cleanliness and psychological bondage with their parents, brothers/sisters, peers and relatives, and also revealed their understanding capacity, learning ability, interests, social responsibilities on environmental protection and cultural values. These rural children are less privileged due to their family background, economic conditions however they are able to manage and adjust whatever is available.

More focus has to be given for the schedule caste children who are really underprivileged and the self discipline should be adhered from the childhood. Parental education and more awareness training should be imparted to them frequently.

In order to enhance the children's behaviour there is a need for co-operative efforts from parents, educators, teachers, Government, NGO's and health care providers to establish the best children to form a better society with good behaviour children.

## REFERENCES

Aggarwal J.C., (2009), Essentials of Educational Psychology, Second Edition, Vikas Publishing House Pvt. Ltd., Noida (UP).

Arthur T.Jessild, Charles W.Telford. James M. Sawray (1978), Child Psychology, Seventh Edition – Prentice Hall of India Private Limited, New Delhi.

Charles Fox, (2003), Educational Psychology—It's Problems and Methods, Sonali Publications, New Delhi.

Chuhan S.S., (2007), Advanced Educational Psychology Seventh Edition, Vikas Publishing House Pvt. Ltd., Noida (UP) Gupta D.K., (2009) Child Psychology, Omega Publications, New Delhi.

Elizabeth B. Hurlock, (1978) Child Development; Sixth Edition McGraw – Hill Series in Psychology.

E.Mavis Hetherington & Ross D. Parke. (1987), Child Psychology – A Contemporary View Point. Third Edition McGraw – Hill International Editions – Psychology Series.

Henry Clay Lindgren (1972,) An Introduction to Social Psychology, Second Edition – Wiley Eastern Limited – New Delhi. p. 249.

Laura E.Berk (2002), Child Development, Sixth Edition, Prentice Hall of India Private Limited, New Delhi.

Richard D.Gross (1993), Psychology – The Science of Mind and Behaviour, Second Edition, Hodder & Stoughton London, p. 403, 431.

Robert I. Watson (1959), Psychology of the Child – Personal, Social and Disturbed Child Development, North Western University, John Wiley and Sons, Inc.

## Journals

The Nurse International – Vol. 4, No. 1 January-February 2012 (www.thenurse.co.in)

Social Welfare Vol. 56, No. 2, May 2009. Children without Childhood – Global Scenario; Dr. Dhruv Tonwani (p. 34).

## Websites

http://www.globalissues.org/print/article/715

Top 10 Terrible Issues Facing Children Worldwide http://listverse.com/2009/07/06/top-10-terrible-issues-facin.

Issues Children Facing in India | TrueIndia Blog http://www.trueindia.org/blog/2010/05/16/103/

Prevalence of Behavioural Problems in School Going Children http://www.iacp.in/2009/06/prevalence-of-behavioural-problems.

Prevalence of Behavioural Problems in School Going Children http://www.springerlink.com/index/H74303488J626864.pdf

Prevalence of Behavioural Problems in School Going Children http://www.iacp.in/2009/06/prevalence-of-behavioural-problems.

http://www.unicef.org/

http://india.gov.in/

www.patient.co.uk/.../Common-Behavioural-Problems-in-Children

# Problems of Street Children in Africa

– Santosh Kumar Mishra

***Key Words:*** Street children, Africa, poverty, family, government response, family life, economic hardship, and employment.

## Introduction

"*Street children*" a term used to refer to children who live on the streets of a city. They are deprived of family care and protection. Most children on the streets are between the ages of about 5 and 18 years old, and their population between different cities is varied. Street children live in abandoned buildings, cardboard boxes, parks, railway, bus stations and footpaths.

Children on streets are becoming too numerous in Africa. This is due to several factors like lack of social and political interest to protect them as the future for the national development. This paper aims to examine Africa's response to the growing problem of street children. Taking Tanzania as a case study, it looks into initiatives that have been and are being taken by various segments of the community to address the problem of street children. The subject areas covered in this paper include:

- What kinds of policies and strategies are African governments putting in place, what are the family and community doing?
- To what extent are families, schools and individual members of society dealing with the problem?
- How is the government dealing with the increasing numbers of unsupervised children living alone in urban streets?
- What role can non-government organisations (NGOs) and community-based organisations play in addressing the problem of street children?

## Definition of Street Children

The definition of street children, for the purpose of this paper, is that of children under the age of eighteen who spend most of their life on the streets. There are those who live permanently on the streets (*"children of the street"*). They live and earn their living on the streets. There are also those who earn their living on the street but do not necessarily live on the streets. They spend most of their time on the street but usually return to some form of a *"family unit"* where there is some kind of supervision or control. This group includes an increasing number of school children that spend most of the day on the streets. All these are considered as street children in this paper.

However, street children may be defined using the following parameters proposed by UNICEF:

- they live in town;
- family ties are weak where they exist;
- children develop survival strategies;
- the street is their main place of stay and replaces the family as a place for socialization; and
- children are exposed to specific major risks.

*"Children of the street"* should be distinguished from *"children on the street"* who work on the street and return home daily to their families. *However,* they share common characteristics related to life on the street. They develop survival strategies because the street provides them with the resources they need, though the onus is on them to benefit from these resources by taking initiatives, as well as dynamic actions to remain alive and by protecting themselves against likely threats.

**Looking into the Contributing Factors**

Not enough is being done to address the problem of street children. Indeed, the issue of street children remains an ignored tragedy that is set to have a devastating impact on the development of African counties. The response to the problem has at best been muted and remains ignored or sidelined by the government and the general public. Key players who are supposed to play a leading role in finding a solution to the problem have become the major source of the problem. Government policies are contributory factors to the persistent state of poverty and increased hardship children face. The family, which is supposed to be the bedrock of children's welfare and protection, is today becoming a major cause of the problem of street children. Parents are sending their children into the streets to:

- beg
- steal or
- engage in petty trade.

Children are leaving their homes to escape domestic violence or because of the breaking up of family structures. Schools are turning into centres of violence and crime and creating an environment to puts more children on the streets.

The general public pretends not to notice the plight of an increasing number of destitute children on streets. The government and the community in general need to put in place viable policies or strategies that will ensure that the plight of street children is urgently addressed.

***"Many of the Children End up on the Streets as a Result of Rural Poverty"***

## The Extent of Problem

When one passes through a market or past a hotel or at the roadside of any major street in the centre of most African capitals, towns or urban areas, one cannot fail to see street children. They are stopping cars and people to beg or to ask for work. One will see others shining shoes, selling sundry articles of uncertain origin, or hurrying to wash the windscreens of cars stopped at traffic signals. Yet others would be roaming around or gathered in small groups waiting for something to do. Their faces show strain and sadness, their clothes are ragged and dirty, others appear hungry suffering from ill-health and malnutrition. There is something mature beyond their years in their haunted expressions. At night, one can see them huddled along street corners, in doorways, or in any dry and secluded corner. They are the representatives of a growing multitude of children who have become known as the *"street children"*.

The problem of street children is a growing problem worldwide, more so in African countries. The presence of large numbers of children sometimes as young as three on the streets in urban areas was virtually unheard of prior to the transition to a market economy. It is now a growing problem in most African cities and towns. The problem requires urgent attention as it threatens the very fabric of society. A starting point would be to get an understanding of who these children are and the factors that turn them into street children.

*"A Large Number of the Street Children are High on Drugs"*

## Highlights of the Problem

One main characteristic of the *"children of the street"* is that they live alone in streets, without proper or reliable shelter. They have lost contact with their parents and, as such, they do not enjoy:

- parental protection;
- love; and
- care.

Street children share the streets with millions of adults, many of whom regard them as nuisances, if not as dangerous mini-criminals. What most of these children actually do on the streets is, of course, work. Children who live and work on the streets often come from slums and squatter settlements, where poverty and precarious family situations are common, where:

(a) schools are overcrowded and poor; and

(b) safe places to play simply do not exist.

Yet other children come from middle class or well to do families who run away from their homes. The number of street children has increased in places experiencing armed conflict, like Freetown (Sierra Leone) and Monrovia (Liberia), where parents or caretakers have been killed. Poverty is also forcing an increasing number of street children on the streets. In some instance, it is parents or guardians who send their children to work on the streets to support their families and others are forced on the streets to find food and shelter which is not forthcoming from their families. Street children face untold hardship and danger on the streets:

(a) lack of food;

(b) unhygienic water; and

(c) inadequate health care.

*"Living and working"* on the streets exacts a terrible toll on street children. They are often victim of every physical and moral danger and as they grow older they often become a danger to others. After such precarious childhoods, most of them are condemned to spend their lives excluded from mainstream society.

## Why are Children on the Streets?

Today, street children are a major issue. Tomorrow, if present trends continue, they could be blight on urban civilization. For Africa, tomorrow is already here. Street children are not only blight on urban civilization; they pose a serious obstacle to overall socio-economic development in Africa.

The world and Africa, in particular, are witnessing rapid and wide ranging socio-economic and political changes. There is rapid urbanization, run away population growth and increasing disparities in wealth. The introduction of structural adjustment programmes and globalization are changing the very fabric of African society. One of the negative consequences of these changes is the emergence of large numbers of children on the streets. In Tanzania, they are known as *'watoto wa mitaani'*, in Kenya they are known as *chokorra'*, and in The Democratic Republic of the Congo (DRC), they are called *'moineaux'* or *'sparrows'*. By whatever name they are called, what stands out is the sad fact that everywhere, children living and working on the street are ignored, scorned, mistreated and misunderstood by society and by governments.

Identifying reasons for the existence of street children is crucial in finding a permanent solution to the problem. There are those who argue that the emergence of street children is bound up with the totality of urban problems - that the phenomenon is exclusively urban: there are no *"rural street children"*. While it is true that street children are usually found in urban areas, many of these children have rural origins. So the problem extends beyond urbanization. It is becoming increasingly clear that there is no single cause for street children. Some of the children have taken refuge in the city from natural or man-made disasters. Others are the offspring of prostitutes. Handicapped street children, rejected by their families, also constitute a distinct and relatively large category. A number have been disowned by a *"respectable parent"* unwilling to *"acknowledge the embarrassing outcome of an affair"*. In such cases, the children do not in variably come from the poorest families. In West Africa, fieldworkers have discovered street children from various backgrounds, including:

(a) a son of a taxi-driver,

(b) a nephew of a dentist, and

(c) even the grandson of a farmer minister.

In addition to the *'pull'* of the excitement and glamour of living in great cities and the hope of raising one's standard of living, there are also *'push'* factors that increase the migratory flow from the rural areas. In many rural areas, natural increase has pushed the population above the carrying capacity of the land. In parts of Rwanda, for example, where the average number of children per family is eight, the resulting subdivision of the land has made agriculture akin to gardening. Families are, therefore, forced to move to urban areas in search of employment and a way out of the poverty trap. Once in the cities, many families break up with children being forced into the streets.

The increasing numbers of street children also indicate a constellation of other trends, such as cut-backs in government social and educational budgets, as well as the breakdown of traditional family and community structures, which leaves children *'unprotected'*. While all of the above are substantive factors contributing to the existence of street children, increasing mass poverty stands out as a major factor for the existence of street children:

- *It is poverty* that is breaking up homes and families.
- *It is poverty* that makes grownups children turn into sources of income or into articles for sale.
- *It is poverty*, particularly in rural areas, that is resulting in street children.
- *It is poverty* that is turning society into a vicious and uncaring society.
- Street children in Africa are the victims of shortsighted policies, or lack of policies. They are victims of an uncaring community that is increasingly being characterized by:
- poverty;
- breakdown of family life;
- violence; and
- economic hardships.

**Box – 1: The Ten Propositions**

The street child must be regarded as a child, not as a delinquent or an anti-social being, or as someone who is sick.

Every adult must first listen to the child to hear what he or she wants before speaking. The role of the adult is to help the child make the distinction between dream and reality.

It is the street children themselves who decide what concerns them both individually and as a group. The adult makes a simple contract with the child. This contract must be scrupulously guarded: it is a basic necessity, not to lie to the child.

Whenever it is possible, the first principle must be to help the child reunite fully with his or her family. When we find a foster home for a child we must ensure that it is not so luxurious as to make him or her forget what conditions he or she must face in adulthood.

Large institutions are not the answers for street children. We must attach great importance to making sure that street children preserve the values of the streets. Values such as strong will; the ability to make do in every situation; the spirit of initiative; the sense of community with other children.

The street child must be brought up in the beliefs of his or her parents or family. All forms of proselytism are forbidden.

The street child must know that from the first encounter with one of our workers we will never abandon him or her.

*Source*: http://www.cyc-net.org/cyc-online/cycol-0201-shanahan2.html, Accessed on July 06, 2012.

## Consequences

One hundred and twenty million is the number of children who, today, live on the streets in the world, as estimated by joint ILO and UNICEF studies. There are 30 million street children in Africa. This figure increases as the global population increases and as social inequalities and poverty levels rise. Street children have a very visible physical presence, since they live and work on the street. Paradoxically, it appears difficult to provide them with essential services and protection. Another characteristic is the entrenchment of children on the streets and the tender age at which they take to the streets.

Some have stayed in contact with their families and work on the streets to supplement the household income. Others have quit their homes. The majority of these children are boys, as girls appear to bear much longer such situations of domestic violence and exploitation. But once they leave their homes, as is increasingly the case, it is more difficult for them to return.

The unavoidable strategy for survival on the street has given rise to a *"street culture"*. This is a culture of resistance, which leads them to invent a new way of managing their individual course in life, with obvious negative impacts on their physical and mental development.

Once they go onto the street, children become vulnerable to all forms of exploitation and inhuman treatment. Their daily life ceases to resemble anything like childhood, as defined by the African Charter on the Rights and Welfare of the Child. In some cases, the people responsible for ensuring their protection are the very ones who commit crimes against them. Street children are often harassed and beaten by the police and are often imprisoned with adults.

It is also interesting to note that this category of children invokes reactions of scorn in developing countries; these are evidenced by an attitude of labeling which varies according to countries. Labeling is a source of exclusion and radicalization, as treating street children like potential danger leads them to really believe so and to convince themselves thereof.

While on the streets, some take up criminal activities like stealing. This marks the start of acquisitive delinquency, as street children will steal to get food or to satisfy their needs. But the greatest risk for a street child is to become a member of a real criminal gang, which will use him/her for:

- drug trafficking;
- begging;
- theft;
- armed aggression; and
- many other illegal activities.

Then, he/she runs the risk of being caught by forces of law and order and being sent to prison. Throughout the continent, these milieus are still places where children's rights are routinely abused, despite protection measures stipulated by international conventions for the protection of minors in detention.

**Poverty and Street Children in Africa**

Poverty is a major cause of street children. Africa, today, is a continent characterized by extreme poverty. It is poverty that is resulting in children being forced to work on the streets to support themselves and their families. Poverty causes malnutrition and poor health and reduces a family's ability to work, thus, creating conditions for children to move to the streets. More than half of the annual deaths in Tanzania and other Sub-Saharan African countries are caused by infections and parasitic diseases. The most affected are children. It can be argued that poverty is a major cause of street children.

**Breakdown of the Family and the Emergence of Street Children**

The family institution in Africa is going through a lot of upheavals. Fewer and fewer children have stable and loving family environments. Many families have broken up with children left to fend for themselves. Many families are also increasingly characterized by:

- absent parents;
- lack of communication between parents and children;
- alcoholism; and
- domestic violence.

Many children run away to the streets to avoid violence and abuse in the family. It is now common occurrence to hear of terrifying stories of abuse of children by parents or family members. Children as old as three are increasingly being sexually abused, starved and ignored by the family and community at large. Today, it is not surprising to see parents or guardians using force or threats to send their children out to beg, steal and work to earn income for the family. Adults are increasingly using children as sources of income and, thus, violating and denying children their basic rights as human beings.

Reduced income increases the pressure to put children to work to support the family. This means that children will have to terminate their educations. When these children are grown up, because they are uneducated, they are unable to find formal employment. Unemployed and without money, often petty thieves, alcoholics or drug user, they are unable to give their own children an education. For every child in the street, many more are at risk. Among the prime candidates are those from poor families, orphans and those escaping from rural life. Further, the social and economic forces, which push families with children into this downward spiral of marginalization, are depressingly self-sustaining and are transmitted from one generation to another.

## African Governments Response to the Problem of Street Children

Of all the agents capable of doing something about the problem of street children, the state is perhaps best situated to tackle the issue. *However*, part of the tragedy of street children is the way African governments have abandoned them to their fate.

With each passing day, it is becoming increasingly clear that many African governments of countries where the problem is most acute have been unable to give it the attention it deserves, and have unintentionally contributed to its continuation. While it is true that most governments have formulated child development policies, set up departments and sometimes ministries dealing with youths and some dealing with women and children, effective action to address the problem is yet to be taken.

While one can speak of some kind of political commitment on the part of many African governments, very little is being done to address the problem of street children. For instance, Tanzania's political commitment to children has been visible for some time now. Major benchmarks of this commitment include:

- the ratification of the Convention on the Elimination of All Forms of Discrimination against Women (CEDAW); and
- the Convention on the Rights of the Child (CRC).

Others include holding of National Summits for children and establishment of Ministries responsible for children and women's affairs in Mainland and Zanzibar. However, most of the direct actions to help street children are being undertaken by:

- non-governmental organisations (NGOs); and
- religious organisations.

African governments appear incapacitated or slow to address the problem of street children. This, in part, stems from the fact that little is known about street children. Even with a Ministry for women and children, government departments often lack comprehensive and reliable data on street children. A study carried out by UNICEF in 1999 indicated that the literature on street children in Tanzania is relatively small and repetitive (UNICEF, 1999). It is, therefore, very difficult, if not impossible, for effective government action without reliable and up-to-date data. Data on street children is by itself not sufficient to find a lasting solution to the problem of street children. National child development policies and strategies are a necessary requirement. Tanzania has been able to formulate and put in place a Child Development Policy that was adopted by the government in 1996. This document is, *however*, very generalized and fails to identify street children as a special category requiring special attention. There is growing need for African countries to formulate and implement dynamic child development policies.

### Africa is Ignoring the Problem of Street Children

The traditional response to street children by most governments in Africa and elsewhere has been repression. Street children arrested for a minor theft or roaming around are often held in custody until somebody can be found to take responsibility for them. This can take weeks or months. Detention in harsh circumstances is the common lot of street children everywhere. This tells more about the real attitude of governments than any examination of national legislation.

Today, governments are increasingly taking ruthless steps to clear the streets of street children and other unscrupulous characters. They do not offer any viable alternative to the street. Politicians, policy makers, and urban planners seem to be helpless in their efforts to either resolve the problem of or assist street children, and have, to date, failed to prescribe plausible solutions which are realistic, down-to-earth, and concrete. It appears that governments pay lip-service to the idea of improving care for street children, but they are influenced by the commonly held opinion that since street children will inevitably wind up as criminals, there is little use in spending public funds for their support. As a result of this, they have been a target of harassment by law enforcement organisations. There are many cases of street children being beaten by police, detained, and sometimes repatriated to their rural homes.

### Too Little to Make a Difference

Street children tend to fall between various jurisdictions, with neither providing real assistance. The emergence of the problem of street children may itself point to gaps in coverage.

Typically, each Ministry may have far more urgent problems on its hands than street children, and none will be prepared to take overall responsibility. Departments tend to determine and shape their programmes in accordance with the policies they are given. These policies are usually aimed at aiding families and are rarely flexible enough to cope with exceptions.

The Ministry of housing, for example, has nothing to offer street children. *Moreover*, relocating families into cigarette packet-sized apartments does not necessarily reduce the incidence of street children, as Western experience shows. From the standpoint of Ministries of Education, street children are dropouts lacking familial background necessary for them to benefit from education. For education bureaucrats, street children had better leave the field free for those who can benefit from education. Labour ministries consider them untrainable because they lack education and are, therefore, unemployable. Youth and sport ministries see them as unruly spirits liable to damage precious equipment reserved for middle-class children. Health agencies are more useful because street children will not refuse first aid, as they will other offerings from well-intentioned adults. In addition, street children may themselves be a threat to public health.

**Community Response to the Problem of Street Children**

Like the government, the community also stands accused of failing to address the problem of street children. Individuals and societies have failed to live up to responsibilities as parents and as custodians of the young. The community tends to hide its head in the sand hoping that the problem will go away. Unfortunately, the problem is not going away, but increasing to alarming proportions.

Traditionally, in an African society, a child was normally a member of a community and could not be separated from it. This meant that even the entitlement that a child deserves was a community matter. In traditional East African societies, the child was educated and socialized by the community for membership into the community. A child in Africa used to be the responsibility of each individual member of society and, *therefore*, children had no need to fend for themselves. They were loved and cared for by society. Today's children are the responsibility of individual parents and are ignored by the rest of the community.

While the number of street children grows by the day, the community remains silent with the exception of a few individuals and organisations. There is no community outrage to the problem. There appears to be no community pressure that is being applied to force government action to find a lasting solution to the problem of street children.

The community has also failed to organize itself into a dynamic force to encounter the problem. This is perhaps the saddest and most tragic part of the tragedy that is unfolding in Africa.

**What needs to be done?**

The first important step is to realize and acknowledge that the problem of street children is one of the most burning problems and challenge facing the African continent. There needs to be a firm commitment by all concerned parties to tackle the problem and not just ignore it hoping that it will go away or that other people are going to come to solve the problem.

Children living on the street, without homes or families, pose the greatest challenge in terms of rehabilitation, often needing long-term one-on-one counselling. Preventive measures are, therefore, vital to protect children from the risk of full exposure to life on the street.

It is suggested that The Union Constitution should be amended to guarantee children's rights. There is no doubt that there is an urgent need for the Government to review the existing law and enact a specific Child Act to ensure the protection of child rights in Tanzania. This also goes for other African governments. Street children are, indeed, a special group of children needing special protection. The legal system must cater for the special interests of children. For instance, children should not be locked up in the same jail as grown up prisoners. The police force needs to be trained to protect street children rather than being a force to harass and punish these street children who often find themselves on the streets for reasons not of their own making.

Education is also seen as a means of helping children on the streets. Most of the street children are illiterate with no basic skills to help them get proper jobs. Education may help break the vicious circle of marginalization and help potential street children towards a better life. This is not proving to be the case for many African countries. With liberalization and reforms, schools seems to belong to a different world, remote from the everyday existence of those most deprived. School then becomes for street children only another possibility of failure. The number of dropouts is inevitably very high, and very few African countries have been able to give further attention to those who have failed to clear the first hurdle. Vocational training must be made accessible to street children as a means of getting them of the streets.

It is often pointed out that the content as well as the form of education is often questionable and unsuited to the needs of the poorest. It is still based on Western middle-class values, promotes a model of consumer society, and reflects the idea that only white-collar jobs are entirely proper. For those weeded out of school, there is no future.

When confronted with the years of wasted effort, frustrated youngsters tend to reject the entire system, and seek refuge among those already in the street. In Africa, where learning carries great prestige, drop-outs have been known to wash windscreens rather than face the shame of returning home to the village. So the issue is not only providing education and training, but also relevant education that will be able to help street children and other children as well meet their most basic needs. It must also be said that street children cannot be motivated to educate themselves while they remain hungry, homeless and in poor health. Therefore, education must be accompanied by adequate welfare for these children.

### Strengthening the Family Unit

Another way to lessen the incidence of children winding up on the streets is to strengthen the institution of the family. As the basic component of society, the family has hardly ever been given adequate recognition by governments. Paradoxically, it is only recently when it is most threatened, that its natural virtues are being rediscovered. Although many governments have developed policies aimed at assisting the elderly, the unemployed or single working women, few have focused specifically on strengthening the cohesion of the family as a component of development strategy.

Policies centreed on the family can counteract the unanticipated side-effects of development, often caused by "*uncoordinated government policies*". As a recent United Nations study on youth maladjustment put it: "*If one conclusion has to be drawn from our data it would be this: juvenile delinquency is not the inevitable result of poverty and rapid urbanization. The intervening variable is the strength of adult-child relationships, most notably family relationships*". A sound policy for strengthening families would recognize the family as the basic unit for the human development and would seek to assist it to cope with change by allowing better access to services such as: (a) *day-care,* and (b) *pre-school education.*

But families cannot be strengthened in the midst of poverty, human degradation and destitution. Neither can families become pillars of strength in face of increasing injustice, inequality and income disparities. The problem of street children will become less pronounced if families and countries could overcome poverty. Justice and equitable distribution of resources is likely to have a positive impact on the problem of street children. At the level of the family, parents and guardians must take responsibility for their children by providing a conducive environment free of neglect, violence and abuse. The shameful exploitation of children by parents and their families can only lead to more children on streets. Collaboration between parents, schools, the community and government will lead to viable solutions to the problem of street children.

### Box – 2: Mary's Story

The old dilapidated train station in the Central Business District (CBD) of Accra is home to several homeless people including street children. The population is made up of disabled beggars, hard drug users, and petty traders among others. The crowded nature of this community makes it ideal for pick-pockets and swindlers. Everyone makes their presence known by selling what they have to make a living.

Street Girls Aid met 17 year old Mary here. She had been living in the station for over 3 years since she left her home in Akyensu, in the Ashanti Region of Ghana aged 13. She'd left due to disagreements between her parents over who should take custody of her and her four siblings. In 2009, when Rose, a street worker at Street Girls Aid, met Mary, she was pregnant and looking very pale. She also had sores on her lips and refused to talk to Rose. It took several meetings and reassurance before Mary agreed to go to the hospital. She said: *"my boyfriend beats me up almost every day and he does not want me to talk to people. I sometimes go hungry because he does not give me money for food"*.

At Street Girls Aid's House of Refuge, Mary received information about nutrition for herself and her baby and accessed basic health care. With support from Street Girls Aid (S.Aid), Mary's baby was delivered safely and she learned how to take care of him. Her little boy is now attending S.Aid's "Railways" crèche daily, while she goes out selling sweets to earn an income. At the refuge, she met other girls supported by S.Aid learning vocational skills and decided she wanted to do that too, so she would no longer be dependent on her boyfriend for survival.

Mary says: *"I now feel I can work and survive without Annor (her ex-boyfriend). He is too domineering."* Her decision to walk away from the abusive relationship resulted from her contact with S.Aid and her experiences at the House of Refuge where she realized that she could achieve her dreams without relying on her boyfriend. Mary looks forward to joining her family one day, but not until she becomes a successful dressmaker, owns a shop and trains many apprentices. She has registered to be part of the next group of girls to participate in the sewing programme at S.Aid.

Mary is very assertive and has a great sense of humor. Since leaving her boyfriend, she has begun describing herself as a 'divorcee'. No one knows what would have happened to Mary if she hadn't left the streets and her boyfriend behind; but what is certain, is that S.Aid provides opportunities for girls like Mary to live with dignity and achieve their dreams.

*Source*: http://www.streetchildafrica.org.uk/pages/marys-story.html, Accessed on July 05, 2012.

**Role of NGOs in Addressing the Problem of Street Children**

In recent years, innovative work for street children has been almost the exclusive preserve of the private sector. In many of the worst affected countries, notably Brazil, NGO projects, executed mostly by religious groups, have developed new ways to help street children. Their programmes are:

- less expensive;
- more humane; and
- more affective alternatives to institutionalization.

Whether the political will exists to duplicate these innovative programmes is another matter. While NGOs are to be applauded in their efforts to address the problem of street children, there is need to scrutinize the role of many of these NGOs and the extent to which they contribute to solving the problem of street children. There are, to date, an increasing number of international and local based NGOs with the supposed aim of helping and protecting street children. Indeed, the welfare of children and their rights is a fast growing industry attracting huge amount of money aimed to go towards improving the welfare of children in Africa. The reality is often one in which many of these NGOs do not advance the interests of children. Money is often diverted to other activities instead of addressing the needs of children. For instance, many NGOs solicit and receive money to help street children or disabled children but end up using most of the money for administrative services. There is, therefore, need to clearly define the role of NGOs in addressing the problems of street children and the welfare of children in general. A code of conduct based on ethical considerations for children is necessary if NGOs are to assist in the advancement of children's welfare.

### Finding Gainful Employment to Street Children

In practical terms, there is a need to legitimize and further develop the concept of street education, which aims at restoring street children's confidence and rebuilding their contact with society. Opportunities for formal and non-formal education and apprenticeship training (such as those offered by Uganda's Africa Foundation and the Undugu Society of Kenya) offer hope for a better future. Also, the affected communities must be sensitized to the plight of street children and galvanized for action to do something about the situation. Even the most poor, given relatively modest inputs of technical advice and finance, can successfully address this task. The goal is for the street children to learn that even if they do not have loving families able to give them the help and protection they need, they do have caring communities. *In addition*, ways must be found to restore the sense of cohesion and solidarity which previously existed in traditional societies.

**Box – 3: Naomi and Derek, Accra, Ghana**

Naomi is from the Northern region of Ghana. Like so many girls in the North, her parents could not afford to keep her or send her to school. When she was just 13 years old her parents found her a domestic work place in a house towards the south of the country. The employers agreed that in return for her work, she would be sent to school and would have board and lodging. Naomi set off on the long trip, and arrived at her new home. Sadly, she never saw the inside of the classroom. The master of the house soon started to sexually abuse Naomi and after a while, she fell pregnant. When she told her employers, the man denied all knowledge and she was thrown out of the house. With no money, and the shame of the pregnancy stopping her from going home, she took to the streets of Accra and started to beg in order to get food.

She was found by one of the workers from Street Girls Aid on the streets of Accra, and was offered a place to stay and prepare for the baby. Inside the House of Refuge, Naomi spent time with other young mothers and set about learning basic parental skills. She had her baby safely in a maternity clinic run by Urban Aid and returned to the house of refuge with her new son, Derek.

S'Aid's workers have been in touch with her family and have explained Naomi's situation to them. When Derek is a little bit older they will return them to her home town. Naomi still hopes to return to school. She has learnt essential skills at the centre, which will enable her to earn some money. Naomi would like the man to take some responsibility for her baby. A dream that is unlikely to be ever realized.

*Source*: http://www.streetchildafrica.org.uk/pages/marys-story.html, Accessed on July 05, 2012.

Resources to help street children can be found in unsuspected corners of society. The elderly, who have leisure time, have great potential. Voluntary action by other age-groups such as youth movements can release well-springs of inspiration and care. Even the disadvantaged themselves can become protagonists of their own advancement. By surviving, street children show positive qualities which, if directed towards positive goals, can break the tyranny of the peer group.

Many institutions, such s universities and technical institutes, represent great concentrations of financial and intellectual capital that are insufficiently concerned with the human problems on their own doorsteps. They should be enlisted in the struggle to help street children. These institutions can assist by collecting and analyzing data on street children. Reliable and comparable data on the extent and nature of the problem of street children are a key element in the effort to eliminate the problem, and effective solutions cannot be fashioned without such information.

Governments, communities, NGOs and UN agencies must together create a system of data collection that will quantify the numbers of children living and working on the streets. In this context, the participatory learning and action techniques, *involving community members in assessing and devising solutions to the problem of street children,* need to be developed in each individual country. Most key initiative that need to taken can fall into one of five categories:

- promoting and enhancing the education alternative;
- building on national and international legislation and improving enforcement;
- empowering the poor;
- mobilizing all levels of society to combat the exploitative forms of child labour; and
- campaigning to persuade parents and other community members to show greater responsibility for their actions.

Any comprehensive attack on the problem of street children must, therefore, advance on several fronts. It must aim to:

- *release* children immediately from the most damaging situations;
- *rehabilitate* those children who are released from work through the provision of adequate services and facilities, especially education; and
- *protect* working children who cannot immediately be released, making their life as safe and as conducive to development as possible.

### Box – 4: The Street Children Project

The Street Children Project (http://www. streetchildafrica.org.uk/pages/the-street-children-project.html) is an initiative of the Catholic Archdiocese of Kumasi set up to address the problems of young vulnerable children who are displaced and homeless and living in street situations in the city. The project is managed by the Daughters of Charity of St. Vincent de Paul. Since the organisation was launched in 2005, it has gone from strength to strength and it regularly rolls out training to instruct people how to work with children on the streets.

The Daughters of Charity run a drop in centre in the Cathedral complex, which is open every day during the week. The outreach work of the project focuses on the alarming number of girls in street situations and therefore most of the lessons revolve around what the girls are affected by - for instance hygiene, STIs (sexually transmitted infections) and pregnancy. The trained workers meet the girls on the streets and offer them the chance to visit the centre, where there are a number of facilities and the opportunity to rest in a safe environment, away from the streets.

The Street Children Project has recently started up two crèches for the children of the street mothers, to provide a safe place for them to be while their mothers go to work. The crèches daily take in 26 children under the age of 6. These children are indeed the lucky ones and are prepared for the exam they take aged 6 to enter into formal education. This exam is standard practice in Ghana, and children are expected to know their alphabet and be able to recite a song and a poem before they are accepted to schools.

In addition to the drop in centre and the crèches, the Street Children Project also runs an outreach programme. Every day workers visit the streets to

> reach out to the girls who live there, and twice a week they conduct a night visit; both to the streets where many children sleep and to the shanty towns were some girls will club together to rent a tiny room with a hard concrete floor.
>
> *Source*: http://www.streetchildafrica.org.uk/pages/the-street-children-project.html, Accessed on July 05, 2012.

But the most important front of all is prevention: ensuring that new generations of children are not driven to the streets. There is a vast range of ideas about how to tackle the unacceptable problem of street children. The problem is so huge and diverse that multiple strategies are needed.

Any comprehensive attacks on the problem of street children also mobilize a wide range of protagonists:

- governments;
- local communities;
- NGOs;
- spiritual leaders;
- employers and trade unions; and
- street children themselves and their families.

### The Voices of Street Children must be Heard

There is little likelihood of finding a lasting solution to the problem of street children without involving the street children themselves. Very often the tendency has been to formulate plans and strategies for children without consulting them. Families, the government and the community at large must seek out the street children and have a meaningful dialogue with them. There is need to speak and listen to the street children in order to help them. There is also need to find out more about their problems and prospects and how the relevant agencies can best help them. Living on the streets is difficult and hazardous and therefore anyone able to survive must be listened to and helped. It is without doubt that street children are resourceful and determined people who must be given a chance. The initial step must be hearing their voices and cries for help. On the other hand, the street children themselves must raise their voices to ensure that their plight is known. They must fight for their rights and the community must help them.

**Areas Needing Special Attention**

Children are Africa's future and Africa must invest in them in no uncertain terms. The presence in cities and other urban areas of large numbers of disgruntled young people can be politically destabilizing. They are prime targets for those prepared to use violence as a political weapon. Street youths-tough, ruthless, unattached, half-educated, intellectually vulnerable and familiar with secrecy, deception and the subversion of authority-can be perfect recruits. The street children and street youths of today can be the guerillas and terrorists of tomorrow. The problem can no longer be ignored.

What is clear is that if Africa is serious in its efforts to promote children welfare it must pay urgent attention to the plight of street children. There is at present no real alarm or outrage from the government or general public on the increasing number of children on our streets. These children face starvation, are at the mercy of unscrupulous individuals and a brutal police force and often die from preventable diseases.

It is argued here that the welfare of children, particularly street children cannot be advanced in a situation of declining human development. It is suggested that African governments introduce measures, which will offset the increasing excesses of the free market economy. The idea of a welfare state, which will oversee the protection of children and other vulnerable members of the society, cannot be sneezed upon. Indeed it is important to highlight that the pioneers and most capitalist of states have in place strong measures which protect children and other vulnerable members of society. The tragedy of Africa is the introduction of crude and unhindered liberalization as a strategy of economic and social development. This trend must be reversed in the interests of our children and future generations.

There is a need for local authorities to shift from their traditional role of providing services along sectoral lines to a more flexible approach based on the perceived needs of urban communities, including children. This implies that various local government committees and departments should be sensitized to understand the connection between various services they provide and how these affect children. The local government should, therefore, assume the overall managerial role of controlling and directing the activities of others in the whole urban development process. This also requires building partnerships with other actors in the city providing community services, e.g., the central government, private sector and NGOs.

## African Committee of Experts on the Rights and Welfare of the Child

The Day of the African Child is celebrated on 16 June every year by the African Union pursuant to resolution CM/Res.1290 (XL). It offers an opportunity to remember the 1976 massacre of SOWETO children, who merely took to the streets to demand their right to racism-free education, in the then apartheid South African.

More than just a commemoration, the Day of the African Child seeks to draw the attention of all actors involved in improving the condition of children on the continent and to unite their efforts to combat the ills that plague the daily lives of children. It is also an occasion for Governments, International Institutions and Communities to deal with this delicate condition of the children by organizing activities to promote the rights of the child.

In the year 2010, African States celebrated the 20th Day of the African Child under the theme: *"Planning and Budgeting for Children's Welfare: A Collective Responsibility"*. This celebration helped in making an assessment of investments in children and of the level of such investment in comparison with commitments by the States to take all necessary steps to give effect to the recognized rights of children. This assessment has shown that a country's commitment to promoting the rights and welfare of children is not dependent on its economic status but rather on its political will and expenditure priorities. Ahead of the 21st Day of the African Child, the Executive Council of the African Union adopted by Decision No. EX.CL/ Dec. 569(XVII) the following theme:

*"All Together for Urgent Actions in Favour of Street Children".*

The phenomenon of children living on the street is a multidimensional obstacle to child development, including at the educational, health and psycho-emotional levels. This is a phenomenon which requires a mobilization of all field workers in a bid to provide multidisciplinary assistance to the children.

**Selected Types of Community-Based Actions**

Actions to be undertaken by the community could include:

- parent-child programmes;
- child-to-child programmes; and
- communitarian programmes.

Parent-child programmes include, for instance, groups of mothers learning the role of pre-teachers to stimulate and educate children at home. As time goes by, such groups of mothers often become active in other aspects of their children's development such as:

- physical health;
- nutrition; and
- social development.

Child-to-child programmes are specifically focused on interaction between children themselves, where the older ones need to learn how to take ownership of a problem in a similar way parents do. Such programmes also serve as a starting point for other activities, e.g., the identification of health problems in the environment and finding solutions to them. These could include lack of safe drinking water, toilets and safe place for children to play. Such activities help children to develop problem-solving skills without waiting for the adults. They could be designed to specifically address lack of adequate shelter and its related amenities, therefore involving children themselves in seeking solutions to their housing problems.

Communitarian programmes could, for instance, include the views and needs of the children in the mutual self-help housing construction/upgrading schemes. In such community-based programmes the importance of collective action becomes particularly pronounced Community members identify their own local needs and thereby provide locally driven-solutions.

Community groups should coordinate their activities and ensure that issues related to the living environment such as supply of safe water, sanitation and housing are integrated to meet the needs of children. They should be able to know what they can do on their own and where they need the assistance of local authorities or other agencies

Community participation has a major part to play in improving the situation of children in difficult circumstances. It may begin with a specific group of disadvantaged children as the point of entry – for instance, rehabilitating street children. Street work is the first entry point to rehabilitation. Community volunteers or households (from where such children come from) develop contact and rapport with the children. The next step is to promote community-based rescue centres where street children are provided with:

- food;
- clothing;
- informal education;
- medical treatment; and
- counselling.

These centres could function as filter points for further referral of children to specialized rehabilitation programmes of NGOs. The programmes could range from education sponsorship, vocational training to projects for disabled and HIV affected.

## Conclusion

The twenty-first century presents a hostile face to many millions of children in many African countries. An increasing number of children are being forced to the streets as result of poverty, abuse, torture, rape abandonment or orphaned by AIDS. Human rights violations against children in the 1990s have become a common and disturbing occurrence in many African countries. Indeed denial of basic human and legal rights including the right to life, liberty and security as a person to children are now a defining feature of the African socio-economic landscape.

The task of helping street children is herculean. It cannot be achieved simply by injections of money, or by merely passing laws. All these efforts may even aggravate matters unless they are accompanied by programmes which will allow children to develop their potential and by a softening of punitive attitudes towards street children by authorities. To sum up, the welfare of children can be advanced in an environment of increasing mass poverty, conflicts and wars. It is in this regard that efforts must be done to ensure sustainable development on the African continent.

## REFERENCES

Amnesty International, (1991), "Human Rights", in Review of African Political Economy, March 1991 No. 50, ROAPE Publications: Sheffield.

Boyden, J. & Gibbs S. (1997) "Children and War: Understanding Psychological Distress in Cambodia", UN: Geneva.

Brett, R. & McCalin, M. (1996) "Children the Invisible Soldiers", Radda Barnen (Swedish Save the Children).

Farmer, P. et. al. (eds.) (1996) "Women in Poverty and Aids - Sex, Drugs and Structural Violence", Common Courage Press: Monroe, Maine.

Freeman, M (1983) "The Rights and Wrongs of Children", Francis Printer Publishers: London.

Gettkart, A. (1993), (ed.) "In the Aftermath of the Earth Summit - Responsible Global Action for the 21st Century", Foundation Development Peace (SEF): Bon – Bad Godesberg.

Honwana, A (1997) "Sealing the Past, Facing the Future: Trauma Healing in Mozambique", Accord No. 3, Special Edition on the Mozambican Peace Process. Coalition Resources: London.

Lugalla, J (1995) "Crisis Urbanization and Urban Poverty in Tanzania: A study of Urban Poverty and Survival Politics", University Press of America: Lanham, MD.

Lugalla, J & Mbwambo, J. (1996) "Street Children and Street Life in Urban Tanzania: The Culture of Surviving and its Implications on Children's Health", Unpublished Research Report.

Makaramba, R (1999) "Gaps in the Law and Policy for the Implementation of the Treaty-Based Rights of Women and Children in Tanzania", Paper Presented at a Workshop at the New Africa Hotel, Dar-es-Salaam.

Maurice, A. (1982). "Underpaid Child Labour and Social Reproduction: Apprenticeship in Kaolack, Senegal". Development and Change, 13.

Munene, J.C. and J. Nambi (1993). "Operational Research on Street Children". Uganda: Department of Psychology, Makere University.

Myers, W. (1988). "Alternative Services for Street Children: The Brazilian Approach". In Bequele, A. and Jo Boyden, eds. Combating Child Labour. Geneva: International Labour Office.

Ojanuga, D.N. (1989). *"Kaduna Beggar Children: A Study of Neglected Children in Northern Nigeria"*. Orono: University of Maine.

Onyango, P., C. Suda and K. Orwa (1991). *"A Report on the Nairobi Case Study on Children in Especially Difficult Circumstances"*. Nairobi: ANPPCAN (unpublished).

Peter, C.M. (1996), "Respect for Fundamental Rights and Freedoms; A New Bill of Rights for Tanzania", in Rugumamu, S. (1996) (ed.) Leading Issues in Development Studies - A Reader Vol. II, Institute of Development Studies: Dar-es-Salaam.

Peter, C.M and I.H. Juma (Eds.) (1998) "Fundamental Rights and Freedoms in Tanzania", Mkuki Na Nyota Publishers: Dar-es-Salaam.

Reynolds, P. (1996) "Traditional Healers and Childhood in Zimbabwe", Ohio University Press: Ohio

UNICEF (1985) "The State of the World's Children 1985", UNICEF: Oxford University Press.

UNICEF (1990) "Women and Children in Tanzania: An Overview", UNICEF and URTZ: Dar-es-salaam.

UNICEF (1994) "The State of the World's Children 1994", Oxford University Press: New York.

UNICEF (1996) "The State of the World's Children 1996", New York: UNICEF/Oxford University Press.

UNICEF (1998) "The State of the World's Children 1998 Report", UNICEF: Oxford University Press.

UNICEF (1999) "Children in Need of Special Protection Measures A Tanzanian Study", UNICEF: Dar-es-Salaam.

UNDP (1992) "Human Development Report 1992", Oxford University Press: New York.

UNDP (1997) "Human Development Report, 1997", Oxford University Press: New York.

URT (1996), "Child Development Policy", Ministry of Community Development Women Affairs and Children: Dar-es-Salaam.

http://cfsc.trunky.net/_uploads/Publications/11.The_Problem_of_Street_Children_in_Africa.pdf, Accessed on May 25, 2012.

http://www.acerwc.org/wp-content/uploads/2011/05/acerwc-daychild-conceptnote-2011-eng.pdf, Accessed on May 27, 2012.

6

# Child Labour a Predicament of the Country's Prosperity

– Goteti Himabindu
– N.V.S.Suryanarayana

## Introduction

Child labour is a very commonplace of occurrence worldwide. Depending on the culture and geographical location, it can be a more widespread problem and can pose particular dangers to younger children. While there are many physical dangers related to child labour, the psychological effects are perhaps an even bigger problem that must be examined. According to the International Labour Organisation (ILO) a new generation of children is being deprived of the chance to take their rightful place in the society and economy of the 21$^{st}$ Century. The ILO has proposed that 'child labour' will disappear in a decade. If this happens well and good. But in reality the situation is worsening. One in eight children in the world is exposed to the worst forms of child labour which endanger children's physical, mental health and moral well being. One of the most problematic aspects of child labour is that it interrupts a child's education and cognitive development. There are children working full-time who do not attend school at all, which prevents them from developing necessary cognitive skills. Even children who work part-time while studying generally perform 12 per cent lower than those children who can devote themselves fully to their education. The percentage is even lower for those children who work full-time and study.

In many countries, children lives are plagued by armed conflict, child labour, sexual exploitation and other human rights violations. Children living in rural areas have fewer opportunities to obtain good quality education. They have less access to services than children living in cities. The UN Convention on the Rights of Children (CRC) (Article 38) has explicitly prohibited person under the age of 18 being recruited into the armed forces or direct participating in hostility. In spite of this special provision under CRC, many countries still involve children below 18 years in hostilities.

While social class and the effectiveness of the child's educational system must be taken into consideration. The effects of child labour become even more pervasive when one considers the negative feedback loop this begins. These young children who work, rather than learn will continue working through the rest of their lives without an opportunity to increase their standing in life. Without the ability to find better paying jobs, due to a lack of education, the workers' children will also be forced early into the workplace to help support their family, ensuring that the lack of education will haunt future generations. Beyond that, forensic psychology dictates that those who live in poverty are more likely to break the law later in life.

Child labour keeps children out of school and is a major barrier to development. To make the anti child labour law a reality, poverty and unemployment need to be eliminated. Unless the standard of living improves at the lower levels of the society, children will be forced to work. Many middle and upper class families do not hesitate to engage young boys and girls to help them with household cores. The middle class family feels by employing a child below 14 years they are helping poor families to increase their earnings for daily livelihood. Working can also impact a child's social development because the child spends time doing labour instead of with peers in social play, learning how to interact properly. Even adolescents who work are impacted negatively. Teenagers, who spend more than 20 hours per week working, are at a higher risk to develop problematic social behaviours like drug abuse and aggression. The risks also impact their educational development as they are more likely to perform poorly in school and drop out of the little education they are privy to.

Child labour also affects the overall social development of children, since they do not get to spend time with others their own age or even enough time with family members. Children need to build personal positive relationships in order to thrive and feel confident. Spending long hours at work, even part-time, prevents the children from properly developing these relationships, leading to insecure adults who are also at risk for other emotional problems. Children who work also experience isolation and depression, which often prevents them from continuing to develop healthy emotions as they grow, and can lead to many physical effects. They are at higher risk for developmental delays as a result of the high health risks both from dangerous working conditions and from taking on physical tasks that are too advanced for them. Children who labour intensely are often smaller than those who are allowed to play and grown naturally. They are also at a higher risk for illnesses such as respiratory illnesses and are exposed to harmful chemicals that can also affect their physical development. Often, these children also suffer from malnutrition which leads to other serious health and mental conditions later in life.

**Age of the Child**

According to the Convention on the Rights of the Child article (i) defines "The child as every human being below the age of 18 years unless under the law applicable to the child, majority is attained earlier". The Indian Penal Court (IPC) defines the child as being 12 years of age. Indian Traffic Prevention Act 1956 defines a "Minor" as a person who has reached the age of 16 years. Section 376 of IPC which punishes the perpetrators of the crime of rape defines the age of consent to be 16 years of age. Section 82 and 83 of the IPC states that a child under the age of 7 years cannot be guilty of an offence and further a child under 12 years is not considered to have attained sufficient maturity to have an understanding of the nature of the Act and the consequences of his conduct. Juvenile justice Act, 2002 defines a male minor as being below 16 years and a female minor as being below 18 years of age. From the above definitions, it could be seen, in the Indian context the age of an Individual in order to be determined as a "Child" is not uniformly defined. The consequences of this are that it offers various gaps in legal procedures which are used by the guilty to escape punishment.

## Indian Scenario of Child Labour and Legislation

According to the UN study, about 150 Million children of age group five to 14 are working in various industries in India. They are found working in road-side restaurants, tea stalls and shops, at construction sites and in factories. Girls suffer labour exploitation to such a degree that million of girls die before they reach the age of 15. They are paid a pittance as low as Rs. 20 per day and many live in shops or work places where they are subjected to various forms of exploitation. Besides the work they are abused physically, mentally and sexually by the scurrilous task masters.

Mafia gangs bring children for "Begging" in urban cities. A child beggar of aged between five and ten collects the maximum. With a burn scar or decapitation they can earn more. As they grow older their earnings decrease. As a consequence they graduate to be big-time traders involved in drug peddling, pick pocketing, robbery and prostitution. A child beggar will only be paid 10 per cent of his earnings of Rs.300 to 500 a day. If he fails to meet the target fixed by the contractor he is punished brutally. The girls by the time they reach 13 years switch over to prostitution. Begging is used as a profession by antisocial elements forcing children in begging. Begging is prohibited in some cities of India by local governments.

The Indian government ratified the UN Convention on the Rights of the Child in 1992 and introduced various pieces of legislation to curb child labour. The Labour Ministry of India has imposed a ban on children under age 14 from working as domestic help in hotels. Under this law any employment of children under 14 will invite imprisonment up to two years and a fine of Rupees twenty thousand. India has also banned employment of children in hazardous industries including the manufacture of fire crackers, carpet making, glass making etc. Under Child Labour Act, 2002. Although India has the second largest child population in the world, there is no single unified separate legislation to deal with all the offences against children. It is high time India introduced an all encompassing common act to safeguard the rights of a child.

## Impact of Child Exploitation on Children

Employing children for labour is an act that endangers a child's physical/emotional health and development without giving the child an opportunity for good education, food and shelter. Of the four major types of child abuses, physical, sexual, emotional and neglect, child labour falls under neglect exploitation and emotional abuse. Child labour is the exploitation of children for commercial reasons. Neglect is a different concept to exploitation and constitutes a failure to provide for a child's basic need. The forms of neglect include physical, educational and emotional. Physical neglect includes inadequate provision of food, housing and clothing, denial of medical care and inadequate hygiene. Educational neglect is the failure to enrol a child at a mandatory school age in school.

Emotional neglect is the lack of emotional support such as the failure to provide psychological care, domestic violence and allowing a child to participate in drugs and alcohol abuse.

A child worker becomes alienated from the rest of the family, has low self esteem, and is likely to engage in self destructive behaviour. He or she is likely to have impaired psychological development and develop anti social behaviour including lying and living with fear complex.

**Can't we stop child labour ?**

A million dollar question with no specific solution. All sections of the society need to work together to stop misuse and abuse of children. Stakeholders to tackle these issues include:

1. National Governmental agencies
2. Non governmental organisations. (NGOs)
3. People's forums
4. Corporate entities and
5. Individual social service activists

Let us analyze why child labour is in existence in spite of various pieces of legislation. Poverty is the major cause for children being sent to work. The percentage of the Indian population living in poverty is high. It is estimated 37 per cent of the urban population and 39 per cent of the rural population is living in poverty. Poverty has an obvious relationship with child labour. The hardships arising out of abject poverty coupled with vices like drugs and alcoholism compel illiterate families especially in rural areas to initiate their children into back breaking work under tiring and sometimes dangerous conditions. The childhood of many children is shattered in the sinks of city hotels, dusty construction sites, hazardous factories and in waste heaps.

The second reason, especially in India, is lack of educational facilities is in some parts of rural India e.g. Bihar, West Bengal etc. where abject poverty still exists. The third reason is the migration of adult labour with their children to urban towns where construction work is booming and plenty of job opportunities exist for poor families including children who are exploited and paid poor wages. Abject poverty and the lack of social security network systems are the basis of an even harsher type of child labour – bonded child labour. The bonded labour system is still prevailing in some states of India where poor peasants who owe money to land owners agree to give their children as bonded labour for long periods. In return they receive a one time payment or waver of their loans. Influential mafia groups are also engaged in trafficking children from remote rural areas to affluent towns. The children are then forced into labour and begging. Girls are forced into prostitution.

## Role of Stakeholders in Stopping Child Labour

1. **National Government Agencies**

   (a) National Agencies need to ratify the UN Convention on the Rights of the Child (CRC).

   (b) An effective legal system needs to be introduced to check employment of children below 14 years through proper legislation.

   (c) Economic sanctions to be enforced on countries that allow the employment of children for the manufacturer of export products.

   (d) Proper monitoring and implementing authorities to be set up to implement various acts passed by the National Government.

   (e) National social welfare schemes to be introduced to supplement income for poor families whose children are removed from work sites.

2. **N.G.Os**

   (a) NGOs have a key role in raising awareness and informing people about the misuse of children, denying them the fundamental rights of shelter, food and education. UNICEF has clarified the role of NGOs as essential players in many of the intervention stages with direct involvement in identification and rescue operations.

   (b) Assist governmental agencies in implementing various pieces of legislation.

(c) Identify areas where child labour exists and bring to the notice of Government.

(d) Undertake advocacy with national governments for the implementing of strict legislation to ban child labour.

(e) Organise rehabilitation centres to shelter children removed from work sites.

3. **Corporate entities**

(a) Include banning of child labour in their mission.

(b) Introduce welfare schemes for children.

(c) Allot separate welfare funds as part of corporate social responsibilities to help organisations working for the cause to ban child labour.

(d) Put up hoardings giving messages on the benefits of banning child labour.

4. **Civil Society/Peoples forum**

(a) Civil society can play an active role in identifying and alerting authorities to child labour sites.

(b) Create awareness among parents and the public about the effect of child labour on children.

(c) Motivate parents to send their children to school.

(d) Organise counselling sessions for children and parents.

(e) Organise joint protests, rallies, hoardings etc. against employing children below 14.

5. **Individual social service activists**

(a) Resist any form of child labour.

(b) Openly oppose child labour activities which comes to their notice without any fear.

(c) Be very assertive in expressing displeasure to shop owners and organisations that employ children for labour.

In India there are many International and National NGOs campaigning for the abolition of child labour. A few important NGOs in the field are:

(a) Child right resource centre (CRRC)
(b) Campaign against child labour (CACL)
(c) Child Line

**Conclusion**

All stake holders should jointly resist any form of child labour using what ever means available. A networking of international NGOs working in this field has to be created for advocacy with various departments to ban child labour. International funding organisations have to identify a contact organisation in each country to help NGOs who are working in this field undertaking activities for the banning of child labour and identify national projects to be implemented in a transparent manner with good stewardship.

## REFERENCES

Anderson B., Phillips H., Van J. Zyl, & Romani J., *Estimates of the Percentage of Children Orphaned based on October Household Survey Data*, 1995-1998. Paper Presented at the Workshop on Longitudinal Social Science Analysis, Cape Town, 2002.

Altshuler J. & Ruble D., Developmental Changes in Children's Awareness of Strategies for Coping with Uncontrollable Stress, *Child Development*, 60, 1989, pp. 1337-1349; N Garmezy, Stressors of childhood, in N Garmezy & M Rutter (eds), *Stress, Coping and Development in Children*, McGraw Hill, New York, 1983, pp. 43-84.

Anarfi J., Vulnerability to Sexually Transmitted Disease: Street Children in Accra, *Health Transition Review*, 7 (suppl), 1997, pp. 281-306.

Ainsworth M. & Filmer D., Poverty, *AIDS and Children's Schooling: A Targeting Dilemma*, The World Bank, Washington DC, 2001, <http://www.synergyaids.com/documents/3505_Poverty,_AIDS_Ainsworth.pdf>.

Ansell N. & Young L., *Enabling Households to Successfully Support Young AIDS Migrants in Southern Africa*. Presented at the XIV International AIDS conference held in Barcelona, 7-12 July 2002, <http://www.aids2002.com/Home.asp>; K Ford & V Hosegood, AIDS Mortality and the Mobility of Children in

KwaZulu-Natal, South Africa. Presented at the 2004 Meeting of the Population Association of America, Boston, 1-3 April 2004.

Bradshaw D., Johnson L., Schneider H., Bourne D. & Dorrington R., The Time to Act is now, *AIDS Bulletin*, 11, 2002, pp. 20-23.

Budlender D., *The Debate about Household Headship*, Central Statistical Services, Pretoria, 1997.

Dawes A., The Effects of Political Violence on Children: A Consideration of South African and Related Studies, *International Journal of Psychology*, 25, 1999, pp. 13-31; Richter L., 1999, op cit.

Department of Labour, *Towards a National Child Labour Action Programme for South Africa*, South African Government, Pretoria, 2002.

Frank D., Klass P., Earls F. & Eisenberg L., Infants and Young Children in Orphanages: One View from Pediatrics and Child Psychiatry, *Pediatrics*, 97, 1996, pp. 569-578.

Foster G., Makufa C., Drew R. & Kralovec E., Factors Leading to the Establishment of Child-headed Households: The Case of Zimbabwe, *Health Transition Review*, 7, 1997, pp. 155-168.

Horizons, *Succession Planning in Uganda: Early Outreach for AIDS-affected Children and Their Families – Research Summary*, Horizons Programme, Washington DC, 2003; Human Rights Watch, Kenya: In the Shadow of Death: HIV/AIDS and Children's Rights in Kenya, *Human Rights Watch*, 4A(13), Children's Rights Division, 2001.

Hunter S. & Donahue J., *HIV/AIDS Orphans and NGOs in Zambia: Strategy Development for USAID/Zambia Mission Programming for Family and Community Care of Children Affected by HIV/AIDS*, USAID, Washington DC, 1997.

Hunter S. & Williamson J., 2000, 2002, op cit.

Johnson L. & Dorrington R., op cit.

Johnson L. & Dorrington R., *The Impact of AIDS on Orphanhood in South Africa: A Quantitative Analysis*, Centre for Actuarial Research, University of Cape Town, Monograph No 4, 2001, <http://www.commerce.uct.ac.za/care>.

Kaufman C., Maharaj P. & Richter L., Fosterage and Children's Schooling in South Africa, in L Richter (ed), *In view of School: Preparation for and Adjustment to School and Rapidly Changing Social Conditions*, Goethe Institute, Johannesburg, 1998.

Luthar S. & Zigler E., Vulnerability and Competence: A Review of Research on Resilience in Childhood, *American Journal of Orthopsychiatry*, 45, 1991, pp. 223-235.

Robinson S. & Sadan M., *Where Poverty Hits Hardest: Children and the Budget in South Africa*, Idasa, Cape Town, 1999; R Smart, *Children living with HIV/AIDS in South Africa: A Rapid Appraisal*, Save the Children, Pretoria, 2000.

Nampanya-Serpell N., *Children Orphaned by HIV/AIDS in Zambia: Risk Factors from Premature Parental Death and Policy Implications*, Ph.D., Dissertation, University of Maryland, Baltimore, 1998.

Rabalais A., Ruggiero K., & Scotti J., Multicultural Issues in the Response of Children to Disasters, in A La Greca & W Silverman (eds), *Helping Children Cope with Disasters and Terrorism*, American Psychological Association, Washington DC, 2002, pp. 73-99.

Rammohan A., The Interaction of Child-labour and Schooling in Developing Countries: A Theoretical Perspective, *Journal of Economic Development*, 25(2), December 2000, pp. 85-99.

Shisana O. & Simbayi L., *Nelson Mandela/Human Sciences Research Council Study of HIV/AIDS*, HSRC, Pretoria, 2002.

Wild J., The Psychological Adjustment of Children Orphaned by AIDS, *Southern African Journal of Child and Adolescent Mental Health*, 13, 2002, pp. 3-22.

Williamson J., Finding a way Forward: Principles and Strategies to Reduce the Impacts of AIDS on Children and Families, in C Levine & G Foster (eds), *The Orphan Generation: The Global Legacy of the AIDS Epidemic*, Cambridge University Press, Cambridge, 2000.

UNICEF, *Childworkers in the Shadow of AIDS: Listening to the Children*, UNICEF Eastern and Southern Africa Regional Office, Nairobi, 2000.

# Strategy for Eradication and Elimination of Child Labour

– Y.Sridevi

The problem of child labour may not be a basic disease. It may be a symptom and a clear indicator of the alarming deficiencies of the basic socio-economic structure of the society. But, as the socio-economic development is a very long and slow process, it may take decades to abolish the child labour in the country. During the last few years, pressure to eliminate or atleast reduce child labour has significantly increased and both national and international agencies are putting their best efforts to achieve this. Since the problem is complex and multidimensional, a variety of intervention strategies at all levels become imperative.

After independence, the Constitution of India recognised the need for granting special protection to child workers. In Fundamental *Rights,* specific provisions in regard to children have been made in part III of the Constitution. "The Directive Principles of the State of Policy" also emphasizes this aspect. Several legislations and executive orders have been exacted from time to time. A beginning was made way back in 1881.

India was one of the founder-members of the I.L.O. and was a signatory to the first convention on the prohibition of child labour in 1919. Since then a number of Acts have been passed in India, the latest being Child Labour (Prohibition and Regulation) Act, 1986. The legislation concerning child labour deals mainly with four points:

- Minimum age for employment of children.
- A minimum period of work per day and forbidding work at night.
- Prohibition of certain types of work for children and
- Medical examination of all working children.

**Identification of Child Labour**

Any action plan on child labour should begin with knowing who are the child labourers. Identification of child labour is not always easy. Therefore, the first task for the panchayats is to identify and survey the child labour situation in their respective areas. In this, all three tiers of panchayats – Zilla Parishad, Panchayat Samiti and Gram Panchayats have to be involved. At Gram Panchayat level, a door-to-door survey can be conducted in order to prepare a database on number of children in villages, their status, socio-economic profile of villages, number of schools, primary health centres, village industries and any other source of income. In addition to door-to-door visits, gram panchayats can conduct the survey in gram sabha/palli sabha meetings. These meetings are attended by all villagers who know each other. However, it is important that villagers are told about the benefits of sharing information about themselves and their children.

**Causes for Child Labour**

Child labour is a problem with several dimensions. There is no single determining cause for its prevalence. Some of the causes commonly attributed for the continuation of child labour are:

(a) Poverty, unemployment, unequal distribution of assets and inadequate wage levels of adult workers with more than 30 per cent of them below the poverty line.

(b) Low literacy level of adults in which female literacy is abysmally low, absence of compulsory education, low access to schools along with high dropouts and discrimination towards female education.

(c) Social and cultural factors which forces the continuity of trade and skill in a particular caste or community at an early age, community exploitation resulting in child and bonded labour, social acceptance of child labour, the society showing no general disapproval towards child labour.

(d) Children constitute cheap labour and they are not able to organize themselves against exploitation.

(e) Low health care amongst poor children prevents them from attending school and forces them into child labour.

In sum, child labour is the cause and effect of poverty, illiteracy, ignorance, ill-health and cultural attitudes. Although causes for child labour vary from place to place, in most cases, a combination of some of these factors perpetuate Child Labour. An integrated approach is essential to eliminate this social evil. In the next section, we look closely at what panchayats could do at local level to remove child labour is discussed below:

### Legislative Action Plan

A Child Labour Technical Advisory Committee has been set up to advise the Central Government in addition of occupations and processes to the schedule contained in the child labour (Prohibition and Regulation) Act, 1986 (CLA, 1986). The committee was empowered to undertake reviews and frame rules as necessary to ensure that the work is regulated in accordance with Part III of the CLA 86. Government will also bring forward legislation to delete the provision contained in the Minimum Wage Act, allowing different wages to be fixed for children adolescents and adults.

### General Developmental Programmes

General development action programme, the NPCL envisaged utilisation of Non-formal education (NFE) centres proposed under the National Policy of Education 1986 (NPE). These NFE centres for child labour will be set-up with the involvement of voluntary agencies and Panchayati Raj institution (self-governing organisations with the participation of people's elected representatives. 73rd and 74th Amendments of the constitution, provides a statutory framework for a decentralised democratic policy). It empowers village Panchayats and Municipalities to spearhead the process of development. Thirty per cent reservation for women in these local bodies would advance the interest of women and children. Funds from the National Rural Employment Programme (NREP) and the Rural Landless Employment Guarantee Programme (RLEGP) will be used on priority basis to create the infrastructure for these centres. For continuing education of child labour, who have successfully completed NFE, efforts would be made to link the NFE institutions with the open schools, or with the forward education system. Along with NFE, the NPCL also recommended to the state Governments, to intensify medical inspection of children in the child labour prone areas, especially in the NFE centres. Programmes utilising funds under Integrated Rural Development Programme (IRDP), NREP and RLEGP etc., Meant for poverty alleviation, would be undertaken to generate employment among poorest families, who often are forced to send their children to work for wage/quasi-wage employment in:

1. the match industry in Sivakasi (Tamilnadu).
2. the diamond polishing industry in Surat (Gujarat).
3. the precious stone polishing industry in Jaipur (Rajasthan).
4. the glass industry in Ferozabad (U.P)
5. the brassware industry in Moradabad (U.P)
6. the handmade carpet industry in Mirzapu-Bhadohi (U.P)
7. the Lock-making industry in Aligarh (U.P)
8. the handmade Carpet industry in Jammu and Kashmir.
9. The Slate industry in Mandsaur (M.P) and
10. The Slate industry in Markapur (MP)

The strategy for eradication and elevation of child labour should have the following integrated approaches:

1. *Comprehensive approach:* A collective and all-round effort from the government, N.G.O. social workers, educational institutions, research etc.
2. *Goal-oriented approach:* Setting and working for long as well as short term goals for eradication and/or reduction and elimination of child labour.
   (a) *Long term goals:* Eradication of child labour
      1. Reduction of poverty.
      2. Provision of adequate employment of adults.
      3. Reduction in magnitude of child labour
      4. Rehabilitation programme for displaced child labour
      5. Creating public awareness about child's rights and labour
      6. Compulsory primary education
      7. Adequate provision of educational facilities.
      8. Effective enforcement of law and coverage of children working in an unorganised sector under the law.
      9. Movements of trade union against employment of children.

   (b) Short term goals : To Improve the quality of life of working children.
      1. to improve educational status of working children by providing education at a convenient time and place.
      2. to improve health status of working children by proper nutrition, regular medical check-up.
      3. to improve work conditions of children by adequate light, ventilation, sanitation, proper sitting conditions.
      4. to safeguard children against occupational hazards.

5. to provide adequate and suitable recreational facilities to prevent children driffing into delinquency, vagrancy, prostitution, drug addictions etc.
6. Movement by trade unions to improve working conditions of children.
7. Effective supervisory machinery of government to improve quality of life of working children.
8. Collective efforts from social workers, N.G.O., educational institutions, etc., to monitor and elevate the quality of life of working children.

**National Authority For Elimination Of Child Labour, 1994**

Government of India constituted a National Authority for Elimination of Child Labour (NAECL) in September 1994. The functions of the NAECL are:

1. to lay down the policies and programmes for elimination of child labour, particularly in hazardous employments;
2. to monitor the progress of implementation of programmes, projects and schemes for elimination of child labour, and
3. to co-ordinate implementation of child labour elimination-related projects of the various ministries of the Government of India.

**International Labour Organisations (ILOs)**

International support for the Elimination of child labour got significant boost form ILO and UNICEF in 1992. Two parallel programmes intended to build financial and human capacity of Government and non-Government agencies were started.

1. Child Labour Action Support Programme (CLASP).
2. International Programme on the Elimination of Child Labour (IPEC).

The ILO implements these programmes under the overall guidance and supervisioin of national level steering committees, headed by Union Labour Secretary. The steering Committees has representatives of government and non-Government organisation.

**Conclusion**

Children are tomorrow's citizens and precious national assets – would learn to respect human rights if they are provided with fulfilment of their rights. One of the child rights is protection from exploitation, especially economic exploitation. The clear violation of this is involvement of millions of children in labour force as child labour, mostly in unpaid/low paid forms. Children are exposed to occupational hazards having serious consequences on their mental and physical development. The government has passed Acts and has a special policy for children but it lacks effective enforcement machinery. There is a need to combat poverty and adult unemployment being the root cause of child labour. An integrated, comprehensive goal oriented approach to eradicate and/or reduce and elevate the conditions of working children is required from not only the government but also from NGOs, social workers and educational institutions.

## REFERENCES

Annan, Kofi, A., (1998), "Foreword", *The State of World's Children,* Oxford; U.K., Oxford University Press.

Bellamy, Carol, (1998), *The State of the World's Children,* Oxford, U.K. UNICEF, Oxford University Press.

Bezbaruah and M.K. Janeja, (2000), New Delhi, *Adolescents in India – A profile,* UNFPA, for U.N. System in India.

*Charter for Children's Rights (2001),* http:/www.wca.nic.in/charter Onna.ntum.

*Common Position Paper of the System in India* on "Child Labour" 1998.

*Economic Times, (1985),* High incidences of child labour, 12:228, November, 10., p. 5.

# SECTION – II

## CHILD LABOUR/STREET CHILDREN AND EDUCATION

# Problems of Child Labour and Education of Working and Street Children in Chennai

– G.Sundharavadivel

## Introduction

> *"Hazardous child labour is a betrayal of every child's rights as a human being and is an offense against our civilization".*
>
> –UNICEF

Many of the street children who have run away from home have done so because they were beaten or sexually abused. Tragically, their homelessness can lead to further abuse through exploitative child labour and prostitution. Not only does abuse rob run away children of their material security, it also leaves them emotionally scarred. Many of the abused children in India encounters are traumatized and some refuse to speak for months. To aggravate matters, children often feel guilty and blame themselves for their mistreatment. Such damage can take years to recover from in even the most loving environments; on the streets it may never heal.

A large proportion of the boys and girls in India's homes have suffered abuse. In addition to fulfilling their material needs, we seek to provide a warm and caring atmosphere. Our vocational centres are also safe, fun places where children gain confidence and self-esteem. We run a help line for children in need and our staff are trained by professional counselors as well as have years of experience on how to foster the children's emotional development.

**Child Labour**

Most Indian street children work. In Jaipur, a common job is rag-picking, in which boys and girls as young as 6 years old sift through garbage in order to collect recyclable material. The children usually rise before dawn and carry their heavy load in a large bag over their shoulder. Rag-pickers can be seen alongside pigs and dogs searching through trash heaps on their hands and knees. Other common jobs are collecting firewood, tending to animals, street vending, dyeing cloth, begging, prostitution and domestic labour.

Children that work are not only subject to the strains and hazards of their labour, they are also denied the education or training that could enable them to escape the poverty trap. India provides non-formal street schools to ensure that working children get at least a basic education. We nurture community support for our schools and seek to mainstream suitable children into the private education system. We also provide popular and practical vocational training where older children can learn skills while also earning some money.

**Gender Discrimination**

In Indian Society, females are often discriminated against. Their health, education, prosperity and freedom are all impacted. The problem is worse in conservative Rajasthan than almost anywhere else in India. For example, because girls carry the liability of dowry and leave the family home after marriage, parents may prefer to have male offspring. Many female babies are aborted, abandoned or deliberately neglected and underfed simply because they are girls. This can be seen in the fact that the female mortality rate amongst 0-4 year olds in India is 106 per cent of the male mortality rate, whereas the comparable number in Western Europe is 74 per cent. The rate is 119 per cent in Rajasthan. Further evidence of the imbalance is that the female/male ratio within the general population of India is unnaturally low at 927/1000 and even lower in Rajasthan at 909/1000.

Gender discrimination is particularly evident in education where boys are more likely to attend school and to do so for more years. The traditional place of the woman is in the home and many parents and children consider education for girls to be a waste of time, especially when the child can instead be working or performing domestic chores. The gender parity of adult literacy between men and women is 29 per cent. Child Marriage is another way in which girls are disadvantaged. In addition to limiting educational possibilities and stunting personal development, early marriage carries health risks. A girl under 15 is five times more likely to die during pregnancy than a woman in her twenties; her child is also more likely to die. India emphasizes care and opportunity for girls. There are more girls than boys in our street schools, vocational centres and homes. We also employ many women and do so at all levels up to the founder, Abha Goswami, herself.

## Health

Poor health is a chronic problem for street children. Half of all children in India are malnourished, but for street children the proportion is much higher. These children are not only underweight, but their growth has often been stunted; for example, it is very common to mistake a 12 year old for an 8 year old. Street children live and work amidst trash, animals and open sewers. Not only, are they exposed and susceptible to disease, they are also unlikely to be vaccinated or receive medical treatment. Only two in three Indian children have been vaccinated against TB, Diphtheria, Tetanus, Polio and Measles; only one in ten against Hepatitis B. Most street children have not been vaccinated at all. They usually cannot afford and do not trust, doctors or medicines. If they receive any treatment at all it will often be harmful, as with kids whose parents place scalding metal on their bellies as a remedy for persistent stomach pain. Child labourers suffer from exhaustion, injury, exposure to dangerous chemicals, plus muscle and bone afflictions. I-India provides nutrition, medical treatment, hygiene and reproductive health education to 5000 children yearly in our street schools and homes. We also operate a Shower Bus that regularly visits street points and offers on-the-spot showers and cleansing products. We employ several full-time nurses and have relationships with hospitals that are willing to treat our children for free.

**Homelessness**

Street children in India may be homeless because their family is homeless through poverty or migration, or because they have been abandoned, orphaned or have run away. It is not unusual to see whole families living on the sidewalks of Jaipur, or rows of individual children sleeping around the railway station. Homeless children have the odds stacked against them. They are exposed to the elements, have an uncertain supply of food, are likely to miss out on education and medical treatment, and are at high risk of suffering addiction, abuse and illness. A single child alone on the streets is especially vulnerable. India prioritizes homeless street children. For them we provide: repatriation to their families, temporary and permanent shelter, street schools, vocational training, nutrition, medical treatment, shower facilities and a help line.

**Poverty**

Poverty is the primary cause of the street children crisis. Poverty dumps a crowd of problems onto a child. Not only do these problems cause immediate suffering, they also conspire to keep the child poor throughout his/her life. In order to survive, a poor child in India will probably be forced to sacrifice education and training; without skills the child will, as an adult, remain at the bottom of the economic heap.

The root causes of poverty are beyond a single NGO's power to change, but I-India believes in helping where it can.

Street schools provide some education, as does mainstreaming of children into government schools and offering scholarships to private schools. Vocational training centres are a pragmatic, but powerful, tool to assist children in escaping the poverty trap. Children at these centres learn skills such as jewellery-making and tailoring which can prove more valuable to them than additional formal schooling. The children earn money at the centres alleviates some of their poverty, and encourages the child and his/her parents to choose vocational training over child labour. I-India has also been active in promoting Child Rights.

## Methodology

The sample consisted of 200 respondents (working children and street children), and their parents or guardians randomly selected from Chennai city North Chennai (Mannady, Royapuram, Korukkupet, manali, Villivakkam, ambathur) South Chennai (tambaram, Velachery, Guindy, Chrompet) using purposive random sampling technique. The population includes both working children and street children.

## Objectives of the Study

In general, the study aimed at identifying problems and conditions of child workers, causes and the reasons for their work. The following specific objectives were formulated keeping the board general objectives in mind.

1. To study the social and demographic background of the families.
2. To find out whether there is any association between family size and income.
3. To study whether there is any association between perception of parents and child labour towards education.
4. To study the reasons for the discontinuance of their studies.
5. To find out whether there is any association between discontinuance and awareness of the individual.

6. To study whether there is any relationship between health problems and education.
7. To study whether there is any relationship between the existing educational facilities and drop out.

**Population of the Study**

The sample consisted of 200 respondents (working children and street children), and their parents or guardians randomly selected from Chennai city North Chennai (Mannady, Royapuram, Korukkupet, manali, Villivakkam, ambathur ) South Chennai (tambaram, Velachery, Guindy, Chrompet) using purposive random sampling technique. The population includes both working children and street children:

1. **Working Children:** Those who live with or without parents and do some kind of labour without going to school.
2. **Street Children:** Children who live with or without parents also have no proper shelter or protective environment to live in.

**Construction of the Tools and Data Collection**

Prior to planning the study, the area of study was visited personally and in formal discussions with the child workers were held to have the basic idea of the study. This also facilitated the investigator to assess the likely problems, constraints etc., involved and helped for designing the tools and their contents. Interview schedule was constructed for both children and their parents to collect data from the targets. It was constructed in Tamil, which is widely in use in the area studied. Care was taken to avoid dialectical phrases. Also personal discussions were made with the targets to cross check and to avoid pointed questions which were very much useful to collect the exact answers from the target. The schedule was pretested in order to avoid flaws in wording, order, inappropriate or confusing nature. This study involves a smaller sample of individuals. The results of the pilot study were therefore subjected to an item analysis procedure. Through this process of testing and deletion the investigator was able to obtain a reliable schedule. This schedule was used to collect data from the target. These data were then put through an analysis in order to arrive at final conclusions.

Analysis and Discussion

There are 200 respondents in the study. Children were in the age group between 7 years to 15 years. There were 130 working children and 70 street children.

**Table 8.1: Nativity and Caste wise Distribution of the Sample**

| Nativity | Caste | | | Total |
|---|---|---|---|---|
| | SC/ST | MBC | BC | |
| Villupuram | 30(15%) | 10(5%) | 10(5%) | **50(25%)** |
| Salem | 4(2%) | 69(34.5) | 1(0.5%) | **74(37%)** |
| Dharmapuri | 4(2%) | 63(31.5%) | 2(1%) | **69(34.5%)** |
| Ramanathapuram | – | 6(3%) | 1(0.5%) | **7(3.5%)** |
| **Total** | **38(19%)** | **148(74%)** | **14(7%)** | **200(100%)** |

*Note:* Figures in the parenthesis are denoted as percentage of respective caste in total.

Table 8.1 infers that Most Backward Class (MBC) people remain to be the majority (74%) in this work. It is evident that more people hail from Salem and Dharmapuri Districts (67.5%), which are undoubtedly dry and backward district, people migrate to other districts in search of work.

## Family Size of the Sample Covered by the Study

Family size plays a key role in the growth and development of any society, major belief of the people is that more the number of children greater will be their income. Hence, they prefer to have more children resulting in undernourishment, malnutrition, ill-health and poverty.

## Reasons for Choosing Work

Parents are always blamed for making child workers work rather than to study. On the contrary, the sample studied reveals that there is no compulsion from the parents to work but on the other hand, children themselves accompany their parents for work so that they do not remain idle.

**Table 8.2: Reasons for Choosing Work**

| Reasons | No. of Children | Percentage |
|---|---|---|
| Not to remain idle | 138 | 69.0 |
| Migration of parents for work | 10 | 5.0 |
| Better wages | 47 | 23.5 |
| Parental compulsion | 3 | 1.5 |
| Other reasons | 2 | 1.0 |
| **Total** | **200** | **100** |

As observed earlier, 69 per cent of the children have dropped out of school even before entering the workforce as workers. If they were in school, the parents would have probably not involved these child workers in work.

## Level of Education of the Child Laboureres

In the world of science and technology, it is education that determines the level of prosperity, welfare and security of the people, education is a dynamic agent of social change and social mobility. In this study 55.5 per cent of child labourers do not know how to read and write. The following table indicates the distribution of the sample based on their level of literacy.

**Table 8.3: Child Workers Education Level and Gender**

| Literacy Level | Male | | Female | | Total | |
|---|---|---|---|---|---|---|
| | No | % | No | % | No | % |
| Illiterate | 105 | 52.5 | 82 | 41 | 187 | 93.5 |
| Primary graders | 11 | 5.5 | 1 | 0.5 | 12 | 6.0 |
| Secondary level | 1 | 0.5 | – | – | 1 | 0.5 |
| **Total** | **117** | **58.5** | **83** | **41.5** | **200** | **100** |

The above table shows that a higher level of drop – outs ( 93.5%) before completing primary level. This is an alarming proportion which is a warning signal to the government. There is only one child worker who has cleared 8 th standard who is included in the case studies.

## Reasons for Discontinuance of Education

Child workers are in deplorable condition because almost all are dropouts from the schools and have joined their parents to work. The reasons for discontinuance as reported by the sample are given below in table.

**Table 8.4: Reasons for Drop-out**

| Reasons for Drop-out | Child Workers | |
|---|---|---|
| | No | % |
| Parental compulsion due to home needs | 88 | 44.0 |
| Unattractive school environment | 74 | 37.0 |
| Migration | 31 | 15.5 |
| No school in the vicinity | 7 | 3.5 |
| **Total** | **200** | **100.0** |

From the above table, it is clear that among the reasons for drop outs both home environment and social environment appear to play equally dominant role. Parents stop their children from attending school because of the poverty of the family, large family size or need to take care of siblings. The unattractive environment in the school in the form of poor teaching fear of teacher irrelevant subject matter, absence of play material and lack of place for play are also a key in making children themselves stop going to school.

## Findings and Suggestions

### *Findings*

- There is less degree of association between the perceptions of parents and child workers towards education.
- Family Size does play a role in pushing children to join work force early.

- The method of teaching is not child friendly.
- Because of the frequent migration of the family find it difficult to get their children enrolled in schools.
- Reasons for discontinuance vary from poor accessibility of schools to parental compulsion.
- The null hypothesis is accepted and it is concluded that there is no association between family size and the monthly income.
- There is a significant association between male and female child workers with regard to their level of literacy and therefore the null hypothesis set is rejected.
- There is a significant association between perception of parents and child workers with regard to education.

### *Suggestions*

Studying child labour data and devise interventions that allow for the possibility of children being in school and working.

- Improve the quality of schooling by investing in education so as to increase its value to children and parents.
- Provide subsidies to poor families prone to having working children so they can afford their children's schooling (income subsidies, nutritional supplements).
- Establish partnerships of international organisations dedicated to improving children's lives.

### Conclusion

Child labour is a significant problem in India. The prevalence of it is shown by the child work participation rates which are higher in Indian than in other developing countries. The major determinant is access to education. In some areas, Education is not affordable, or is found to be inadequate. With no other alternatives, Children spend their time working. The state of education in India needs to be improved. High illiteracy and dropout rates are reflective of the inadequacy of the educational system. Poverty plays a role in the ineffectiveness of the educational system. Dropout rates are high because children are forced to work in order to support their families. The attitudes of the people also contribute to the lack of enrollment – Parents feel that work develops skills that can be used to earn an income, while education does not help in this matter. Compulsory education may help regard to these attitudes.

Child Labour cannot be eliminated by focusing on one determinant, for example education, or by brutal enforcement of child labour laws. The government of India must ensure that the needs of the poor are filled before attacking child labour. The development of India as a nation is being hampered by child labour. Children are growing up illiterate because they have been working and not attending school. India needs to address the situation by tackling the underlying causes of child labour through governmental policies and the enforcement of these policies. Only then India will succeed in the fight against child labour.

## REFERENCES

Devi. R, 1985, Prevalence of Child Labour in India: A Secondary Data Analysis, In *Child Labour and Health: Problems & Prospects,* edited by U. Naidu and K. Kapadia, Bombay: Tata Institute of Social Sciences.

Grootaert.C, and R.Kanbur, 1995, Child Labour: An Economic Perspective. *International Labour Review* 134:187-201.

Human Rights Watch, 1996, *The Small Hands of Slavery -- Bonded Child Labour in India.* New York: Human Rights Watch.

International Labour Organisation, Geneva 1992, *World Labour Report.*

International Labour Organisation, Geneva 1993, *World Labour Report.*

International Labour Organisation, Geneva 1995, *World Labour Report.*

Jain. S.N, 1985, Legislation and Government Policy in Child Labour. In *Child Labour and Health: Problems & Prospects,* edited by U.Naidu and K. Kapadia, Bombay: Tata Institute of Social Sciences.

Mehra-Kerpelman.K, 1996, Children at work: How many and where? *World of Work* 15: 8-9.

Nangia.P, 1987, *Child Labour: Cause-effect Syndrome*. New Delhi: Janak Publishers.

Narayan.A, 1988. Child Labour Policies and Programmes: The Indian Experience. In *Combating Child Labour*, Edited by A.Bequele and J.Boyden. International Labour Organisation, Geneva.

Subrahmanya. R.K.A, 1987, Can the Child Labour Act of 1986 Effectively Control Child Labour? In *Young Hands at Work – Child Labour in India*, Edited by M.Gupta and K.Voll. Delhi: Atma Ram & Sons.

The World Bank, Washington, 1995, Economic Development in India: Achievements and Challenges.

Weiner.M, 1991 The Child and the State in India, Princeton University Press, Princeton.

# Non-Formal Education for Street Children

– Uma Joshi

Street Children phenomenon and issues are universally known and recognized. The term street children lead one to think that they are homeless, who have left or run away from home. Broadly speaking, they are the ones who live on the streets or are working most of the time on streets to support their families. Those who live on streets are put off from their families and others are the ones who return home after working on streets to earn. It is observed that generally people have negative perception and attitude towards street children. Further, they are also abused mentally and also physically by the police, their group members or peers and their employers. Street Children are those boys or girls who live on streets and unoccupied dwellings and earn for their livelihood. They are not protected or guided by adults.

USAID has categorized Street children as:

➢ **Children on the street:** Children who visit their families/ return home every day but spend most of the day on the street.

- **Children of the street:** They have no home but the streets and no family support. They move from place to place living in shelters and abandoned buildings.
- **Children of a street family:** A Family lives in the street and children live with their families on Sidewalks or city squares. They work in streets with their families.

Most of the street children are found engaged in some work to earn to satisfy their needs. It creates strain on them and they face all kinds of hazards of their work. The living conditions of street children are miserable. As most of them are homeless, they live and work in dirty and filthy environment consisting of garbage, animals and open sewens. Such conditions lead to their poor health status, injuries, reactions due to working in unhygienic environment.

It has been noted that the causes and characteristics of homelessness in the developing world appear to be more systematic, of longer duration and more permanent than those appear in the developed world. (Irving: 1996: P.297) In developing countries, programmes involving street children are conducted either by government departments or NGOs. Many times street children are held responsible for crimes and thefts that occur on streets or near by places and they are treated as criminals by police. They face inhuman treatment in all walks of their life.

It is estimated that 100-150 million children live and/or work on the streets. Forty per cent are homeless and 60 per cent are working to support their families on the street. (http://portal.unesco.org). In general there are fewer girls than boys actually living on the streets (studies indicate 3% and 30% depending on the country). Street Children are largely boys between the ages of 10-14. (www.amnestyusa.org/children)

"In India, street and slum children are that section of society needing help the most. Orphans belong to institutions which care for them. But they are deprived of all the basic rights that any child should have education, proper nutrition, medical care and a safe clean environment" said Anneta Patel, who is the secretary of Navjeevan Sanstha. (The Indian express, Nagpur ed., 13 April.2010.)

Legislative provisions have been made for the welfare of the street children. Under these provisions, workshops have been organized for Members of Parliament, police, NGOs to sensitize them regarding the issue of street children and what needs to be done. A Goverenment – NGO Project 'CHILDLINE' a 24 – hour, free emergency telephone hotline in 29 cities has been started and it has been used by more than one million children in past five years. Many NGOs have taken up the projects on development of street children.

Regarding the constraints and challenges in dealing with the issue of street children, Rane (2001) pointed out that lack of implementation and monitoring mechanisms for programmes and lack of enforcement of legislation, impact of forced evictions, demolitions and displacement on children, the large number of child labours, wide spread poverty, unemployment, increasing rural-urban migration and attraction to city life pose many problems and hurdles in working effectively for street children for any development agency.

According to child workers in Nepal Concerned Centre (CWIN), established in 1987 works as an advocate organisation on the rights of the child, works for welfare and dignity of street children. They found that the reasons behind being street children have been arm conflict, urban migration, attraction of city, orphaned, abandoned and disability, child labour exploitation, garbage and rag picking, socio-economic reasons, family problems, child delinquency, growing slums and begging habits. It was further reported by CWIN that the problems faced by street children are related to survival, security, police harassment, closeness to the world of crime, emotional insecurity, abuse, exploitation, risk, accidents and street pollution.

Participatory workshops in six divisional cities of Bangladesh identified problems and needs of street Children. These are:

- **Shelter/Security:** Children demand safe shelter because they do not have access to bathing and latrine facilities and are vulnerable to sexual abuse, beating and they are robbed.
- **Decent jobs and income:** Street Children want access to decent jobs and better wages.
- **Health care facilities:** Street Children want access to curative healthcare facilities as they suffer from incidences of cuts and wounds, eye infections, diarrhea, dysentery, skin diseases, hepatitis, fever and other contagious diseases.
- **Education:** Street Children want to be educated in order to get a decent job and be respected in society. (UNDP Sept. 2001.)

It is obligatory on part of the Government and NGOs to implement the strategies that provide protection, education, life skills and opportunities for development. They should be brought into main stream to participate actively in their own development. Gradually, they should be helped to transform themselves in to contributory citizens of the Society.

Mostly, the street children are found to be from the lower socio economic status, who were deprived of educational facilities, or they dropped out due to various reasons. Creating educational opportunities should not be looked upon as a welfare programme but it should be implemented under the right to education provisions. According to Khan (2008) "despite a growing recognition of their vulnerability and disadvantaged status, there have been strikingly limited efforts to improve the condition of street children especially by providing them with appropriate basis education. It will not be an exaggeration that this section of our society has largely remained outside the main ambit of developmental interventions". Their educational programmes should also have the components of community involvement, general education, value education and vocational training along with regular meals and clean clothes. Psychological assistance should be available to those who are without parents, and to those children with dreadful experiences in the streets.

Open school education system should be strengthened and popularized. It's structure should be developed in such a manner that it provides easy access of educational opportunities to the street children. A major role and responsibilities of meeting the needs of the street children lies with the government. NGOs, voluntary organisations, corporate sectors, academic institutions involved in extension/ development work can play a role in implementation of programmes, advocacy, evolving effective strategies for education and development of street children. The educational system for children should provide for flexible schedules and good guidance and counseling services. The educational interventions should help them raise their self esteem and confidence and improve their outlook towards life. Vocational training programmes should be run by the Government, NGOs or they grow as an adult, they are able to earn their living and come out of the poverty. Even if these children are unable to go for formal schooling the vocational skills training alleviates their poverty to some extent. Skill oriented training programmes for street children should be selected on the basis of their viability to generate income.

UNESCO (1995-2011) suggested the following for rehabilitation of street children.

- National campaigns and information dissemination to encourage Governments and civil society in the provision of educational opportunities for all.
- Adoption of a multisectoral approach to promote the right to education and strengthening partnerships between Government, UN Agencies, civil society, NGOs and the private sector.
- Basic service provision (e.g. literacy courses, medical and psycho-social support, food and clothing) provided at street level to aid children in making informed and positive decisions about their lives, about leaving the streets and becoming integrated in residential centres or reintegrated with their families.

- Inclusion of street children in the mainstream school system from early on and rehabilitation programmes for drop-outs.
- After-school educational activities, personalized educational workshops and functional literacy courses and vocational training.
- Organisation of advocacy campaigns and preventive education programmes for street children on HIV and AIDS and development of life skills training.

Rehabilitation of street children should be taken up not only by providing them proper living conditions, but through effective non-formal education programme which enables them to become self reliant and capable of entering in to the mainstream of education. This can also prevent them from exploitation by becoming child labourers or objects of exploitation in future. The Programmes for the street children should be based on their needs with holistic approach where the families support is sustained for reintegrating the children. Otherwise, they may enter again the world of street children. The NFE for street children should start with practical skills training, so that they can earn for their day-to-day living. Provision can be made in formal school system to accommodate street children with Government or NGO assistance. Night Schools and street or pavement schools also can serve the purpose initially and gradually. They can be institutionalized or taken back to their families.

Three major Strategies have been highlighted in the country reports on street children:

1. **Correctional and Curative strategies:** Street children should not be treated as delinquents or threat to society, so that they can be prevented from inhuman punitive correctional methods. It requires educational and developmental approach for their rehabilitation.
2. **Ameliorative strategies:** This focuses on minimizing the negative effects of street life of street children and engaging them in educative and constructive activities with the provision of basic amenities.

3. **Preventive strategies:** This stresses poverty reduction programmes as well provision of basic amenities to prevent children from going to streets to earn for their and them and family's living (info.streetchildren.org.uk.)

India provides non-formal street school to ensure that working children get at least basic education. They nurture Community support for their schools and seek to mainstream suitable children in the private education systems. They also provide popular and practical vocational training where older children can learn skills while also earning some money: (www.i-indiaonline.com/sc_crisis_. the problem.htm).

Street children can be provided residential facility to study, especially those who are homeless. This is because poverty is the root cause of the creation of street children. They have to earn for the family and sacrifice education and other opportunities for their development. The study material and stationary should be given freely. Non- formal education programmes for street children should be based on identified needs of the area in which they are living, so that they have greater employment opportunities.

There should be programmes for the families of street children also to raise their awareness regarding the needs of the children, support programmes for them and the sensitization of the families towards educational and training needs of their children for the better future of their families. The families of street children should be made the beneficiaries of the poverty alleviation programmes so that they do not push children in to earning and allow them to participate in the development programmes for their better future.

## Role of Media

Media should play an important role in sensitizing the citizens and other stakeholders about the problems and lives of street children and causes leading them towards street life, so that they develop acceptance, sensitivity and positive outlook towards them. This will create non-threatening environment for street children. NGOs all other agencies working for street children should develop networks and mechanisms to exchange and share information and project experiences to continuously improve their strategies and for the development of strategies for the development of street children.

**Role of Government and Strategies**

Government and NGOs have programmes for street children but it requires effective monitoring, documentation and suggestions for continuously improved future action. There is a need to create a forum for street children NGOs and their networking for the exchange of data, good practices, exchange of information and advocacy. However, the data and statistics related to street children is not always reliable due to their mobility.

Street children's programmes can be exclusively for them at initial stages but later on they should be integrated with the programmes for other Children to promote their normal development. At present except the project teams working for street children there is no systematic involvement of the urban local authorities or other philanthropic groups. There is a need to start special centres of activity as well as out of school education for street children. These centres should be adequately equipped to impart meaningful training to them. Such centres can also take care of food, nutrition and health needs of street children. The corporates must be directed by the Government to support such centres under their Corporate Social Responsibility (CSR). These centres should become the channels for transition to formal school. These centres can provide guidance/counseling and rehabilitation services to street children.

The working group at Municipal Corporation level should be formed to address the problems and needs of street children and evolve effective plans for it, with the allotment of adequate funding. There is a need to develop linkages and partnerships amongst and between NGOs, government, Corporate sectors at local, state and national level to ensure development programmes for street children and other vulnerable groups so that they are not marginalized or deprived of their basis rights.

The laws related to juvenile delinquents must be reviewed and made child friendly in which the punishment leads to the development of a child. Thus, the educational programmes for street children should basically focus on provision of basic needs, school integration, vocational training, guidance and counseling services and scholarship. Street youth who complete the education and training successfully should be given financial support in the form of loan so that they can start some work to earn.

Academic institutions engaged in training in development practice should develop learning modules and packages for the education of street children, experiment with them and do research to suggest effective approaches to educate them. They can also organize counseling workshops for the parents of the street children. This is important for the adoption of holistic approach to help the street children to be part of the main stream. Parents sensitivity towards their children's need and their care and attention can help a great deal in addressing the psychological, social and cultural trauma.

Sustainable rehabilitation should be through non-formal education which uses the methods like, personal contacts, home visits, group teaching, excursions, audio-visual presentations, role palys, dramas and so on which allow their participation and make learning more interesting. Educational experiences should address the root causes of their problem and prepare them to meet their needs in the problem areas of their life. Street children educators may face problems in offering learning experiences to these children. This is due to the variations in age groups, specific needs, maturity, language, culture and so on. There is inadequate supply of teaching materials for educating a group of street children with such wide variations.

Academic institutions engaged in development practice training can also take up projects on developing tailor made content for educating street children and street educators training programmes. Educational programmes for street children should be supervised for their organisation, and coordination among the collaborating agencies. The focus on child participation by creating child friendly environment in NFE classes for street children is very important, so that they voice out their problems. Such environment can work as facilitator and motivator for children.

## Conclusion

To conclude, having discussed the issues related to the phenomenon of street children, the effective and sustainable way for their rehabilitation and development would be to use rights based, holistic, integrated, family and community based and educative approach emphasizing linkages and partnerships among and between, government, NGOs, corporate sectors and academic institutions engaged in development training. These can go a long way in governing the interventions for well being and better future of street children.

## REFERENCES

Colombo Statement of the Civil Society Forum for South Asia on Promoting and Protecting the Rights of Street Children (2001) Colombo, Srilanka.(Country Reports).

Bhattacharya, M.,(2007) A Saga of Agony and Shame: Child Labour and Child Abuse in India. Decent Books. New Delhi.

Joshi Nidita(2008), Educational Rehabilitation for Child Labourers From Selected Communities of Baroda City. Unpublished Master's Dissertation, M.S.University of Baroda, Vadodara.

Khan, N.A. (2008) Educating Street Children. The Daily Star, Dhaka, Bangladesh (www.asiafinest.com)

Rane Asha. Strategies Adapted to Rights of Street Children in Region. Country Report – India. (info@streetchildren.org.uk) UNICEF, UNDP. Sept. 2001.

Rao. M., (2000) Exploited Children – A Comprehensive Blueprint for Child Labour Rehabilitation. Kanishka Publications, New Delhi.

USAID Epstein Irving (1996) Comparative Education. Vol. 32, No. 3 p. 297 http;//partal.unesco.org www.amestyusa.org/children, the Indian Express. Nagpur ed.13th April 2010. (www.Indian express.com)

UNESCO.(1995-2011) www.i– indiaonline.com/sc_crisis_the problem.htm.

Weiner M. (1991) The Child and Status in India, Oxford University Press, New Delhi.

www.i. – Indiaonline.com/sc_crisis_the problem.htm. NGO's Case Study Reports on the NFE Practices for street children.

# Education and Child Development

– J.Anuradha

## Introduction

Child education is a subject of immense importance as it is the foundation stone for the future. It cannot be ignored completely or even taken lightly. Advanced countries of Europe and America pay a great attention to the development of child talent, they study their psychology, the physical problems, their various handicaps, and the socio-familial problems affecting them. They devise new techniques, newer methods and practices to enhance the development of child and educate them for their future life. Children are the lifeline of our society and our world. They are the greatest natural resource a country has. For our world to be safe and productive, our children must be self-accepting, tolerant of other people's differences and resilient. Parents and teachers have the responsibility for nurturing the kinds of healthy attitudes and skills that children require in order to develop these attributes. For children to like themselves and develop good coping skills, they first need to feel accepted for their own qualities and characteristics and to accept these themselves. When people close to children accept and love children for whom they are, the children are more likely to develop a positive sense of self. Those who can maintain a positive perspective on change and a challenge perspective towards adversity are better able to deal with distress. Likewise, children who are good decision makers not only avoid the consequences of poor decisions but also are able to effectively deal with life's everyday stressors.

India remained in bondage of the British Empire for over one hundred and fifty years although Declaration of American Independence had taken place in 1776 and the National Assembly of France had the courage to adopt the Declaration of the Rights of Man and Citizen in 1789, India continued to live as a slave's life under the British regime before. As a result of the sacrifices made by the sons of the soil, could bear fruit of freedom in 1947 and India became a sovereign, democratic and republic country. Of course, with the dawn of freedom there was reborn the desire to tastes the fruit of human rights which had remain unknown to majority of Indian masses. The time was ripe and the will firm to act. The Constitution of India, which took some time to get its proper shape, was enforced on 26th January, 1950, declaring India to be a sovereign, democratic republic. The Universal Declaration of Human Rights had already been made in 1948, it was in 1950 that India, as an independent nation, could infuse confidence and a sense of free man or woman or child in every heart which took pride in being Indian. Coming to the rights of child labours, under the Bonded Labour System (Abolition) Act of 1976, Rehabilitation of free bounded labourers has been launched. Rights of Child covered under the Article 39(E), restrains any abuse of the children below 14 years of age.

The contemporary concept of human rights presupposes human rights education. This is the reason why every human rights document gives an important place to the right to education. The General Assembly of United Nations, while proclaiming the Universal Declaration of Human Rights called upon "every individual and every organ of society" to "strive by teaching and by education to promote respect for these rights and freedoms..." The rights of the child are concerned with various aspects of the right to education and the content of education including, among others, 'that the education of the child should be directed to the development of respect for human rights and freedoms. Human Rights education, over the years, has become an integral part of the goals and objectives of education. A clear reflection of these goals and objectives can be seen in the first National Curriculum Framework. The National Policy of Education, 1986 strongly favours that the child's right to education and also some of the important rights concerned in the core curriculum for all stages of education.

## Role of Home

The home, it is said, is the cradle of all virtues. It is an informal agency of education. The home plays a significant role in human rights education. The mother is the first teacher of the child. Her attitude towards human rights is very important. If she is favourably inclined to the importance and value of human rights, she will play a vital role in building desirable attitudes towards human rights in children. The way the family brings up the child shapes the attitude of the child. The society has to be enlightened about the rights of the child. Modern child psychology forbids any kind of punishment. The human rights violation is more seen in case of illiterate and poor families. These families neglect the feelings of their children and due to poverty, the children are forced to child labour and the result is that the children become the victims of society. They develop fake feelings towards their family and society as they were neglected. As a matter of fact, the native activities develop in contrast with random and capricious exercise and children are put to direct growth in the society. The instinctive activities may pervert, stunt and corrupt the children and the normal development of the child is affected. They are influenced by many unlearned powers in the society and by their childhood are in great damage.

Rousseau's passionate assertion of the intrinsic goodness of all natural tendencies is a reaction against the prevalent notion of the total depravity of innate nature, and has had a powerful influence in modifying the children's interests. But it is hardly necessary to say that primitive impulses are of themselves neither good nor evil, but become one or the other according to the objects for which they are employed. The neglect, suppression and premature forcing of some instincts at the expense of others are responsible for many avoidable ills, there can be no doubt. But the moral is not to leave them alone to follow their own 'spontaneous development', but to provide an environment which shall organize them. Returning to the elements of truth contained in Rousseau's statements, we find that natural development should enable them to develop thinking in a positive manner. The desirable specific aims according to Rousseau are:

- Natural development as an aim fixes attention upon the bodily organs and the need of health and vigour.
- The aim of natural development translates into the aim of respect for physical mobility. It is to strengthen the body before exercising the mind.
- The general aim translates into the aim of regard for individual differences among children. The difference applies not merely to their intensity but even more to their quality and arrangement.
- The aim of following nature means to note the origin, the waxing and waning, preferences and interests.

Capacities bud and bloom irregularly. We must strike when the iron is hot. Especially precious are the first dawning's of power. The tendencies of early childhood are treated fix fundamental dispositions and condition the turn taken by powers that show themselves later. Observation of natural tendencies is difficult under conditions of restraint. They show themselves most steadily in a child's spontaneous sayings and doings. We must see that the desirable ones have an environment which keeps them active and direct them towards goal setting. In order changes in these children who are in child labour, first the parents and the society must be educated. Co-ordination of school, society and parents is important to develop children as healthy citizens. Therefore, the starting point of all educational reform is the re-linking of the school to the life in the community and activity in the home and restoring the intimate relationship between them. The parents should take pride in educating their children.

"Good parents are made, not born." It is an important responsibility of the school to educate the parents as regards the understanding of the needs of their children. This is of special significance for rural areas. Though this idea does not enjoy due popularity yet the ideal of parent education is beginning to have practical significance in advanced communities. Gandhiji advocated a programme of wise parenthood in his scheme of education. Parent education can be done in school by starting 'Mother Clubs', 'Parent Education Association' and etc.

**Role of Teacher**

One of the characteristics of teaching today as compared to that of a decade or so ago is the greater responsibility of the teacher as a counsellor of youth. Today, in almost all schools, the services of the teacher to young people include various types of activities having for their objective assistance to boys and girls in solving their problems of life which are seldom dealt with in their school subjects. In all schools, teachers have opportunities to render valuable guidance service in relation to the teaching of their school subjects. The following are some of the duties of teachers in school.

- The teachers must be able to give specialized training in personality and temperament for leadership and conflict management.
- The teachers must always be alert and ready to guide children.
- Teachers should prepare children to different competitions and also training must be given in this regard.

- Teachers should associate with young people in their play and social activities.
- The teachers should be as superior counselors in broadening the knowledge of children.
- There must be a co-operative understanding between teacher and children.
- Teachers must strive to improve the attitudes and skills of children.
- Discussions by teachers should be carried out in a spirit of helpfulness and at professional level.
- Emphasize success rather than failure.
- Promote confidence in children to overcome different challenges in life.

## REFERENCES

Bhawan Misra, "Education and Child Development", Mohit Publications, New Delhi, 1999.

Bhatia K.K & Narang C.L, "Philosophical and Sociological Bases of Education", Tandon Publications, Ludhiana,.

Kumar R., "Child Development in India", Ashish Publishing House, Punjabi Bagh, New Delhi.

Ramachandra Rao M., & Dr. Vijaya Lakshmi D., "Psychological Foundations of Education", 2005.

# Promoting Reading Habits Among Rural Children
## *Gri Experience in Dindigul District, Tamil Nadu*

– L.Raja

*ABSTRACT*

This study was undertaken to understand and examine the reading interest among rural children in Dindigul District. It covers the reading habits, problem faced by children, parents and teachers and strategy for enhancing the reading habits among the rural children. It is greatly hoped that the reading habits among rural children needs to be given a proper awareness and motivation so that the rural children acquire a strong foundation for reading. Reading is vital for acquiring knowledge, skills and creating a knowledge society in the emerging areas.

This study was an explorative study among 200 rural children from 2 blocks and 20 children each in 10 villages. 100 parents i.e. (10 parents from each village), 20 teachers' one male and female from 10 villages. Collected data has been tabulated and analysed systematically. The major findings have been drawn from children, parents and teachers from their various reading habits from local news papers, journals, magazines, books and other materials.

The findings have shown that the reading habits among rural children are very less. The parents were struggling to make their children to develop the reading habits because they themselves have lost their track and are unable to read. This sometimes creates a strange relationship between parents and children. Ultimately the children do not listen to their parents to read.

After understanding their problems various strategies have been adopted to enhance their reading habits including establishing rural children libraries and motivating them to gain confidence in day today life through the Department of Lifelong Learning, GRI-Gandhigram. Thus, the role of University helps the rural children to acquire the reading habits and interest to understand the current trends of local and global situation. This study was on the basis of Action Research.

## Introduction

In the computer electrical and electronic age children are mostly affected by TV, Video, Computer, mobile and other electronic gadgets. As a result parents and teachers are finding it very difficult to motivate their children to read their own subjects as well as other books. Therefore, there is an urgent need for understanding the attitude of the children towards reading habits and to find out ways and means to promote reading habits among the rural children.

## Importance of Reading

Reading is one of the very important and most significant in every one's life in the highly upcoming literate society. But still 45 per cent of the rural people are illiterates. On the one hand more and more literacy classes have been conducted by various agencies.

On the other hand the neo-literates are losing their reading habits due to lack of follow-up. Because most of the parents are illiterates and neo-literates and they do not understand what their wards are reading and studying?

All the more it is very important for the parents to make their wards to read and study well so that they will not suffer in their future life as they are struggling for life.

**Problem faced by them**

The children are the most vulnerable target and are greatly affected by the electrical and electronics equipments. The children are having more distractions from these and spoil their creative ideas. Largely children are carried away by the non-stop advertisements and attractive movies.

As a result, the rural children are mostly unable to concentrate in their study, values are forgotten, neglected and it is very difficult to convince the children by giving any kind of counselling and advise.

The peer-group participation, group activities, group games; group interactions are not practised often. The new technology and new culture enters in the minds of the rural children which spoil their mind and study habits.

The children always tend to watch the TV instead of doing their home work as assigned by the class teachers'. Inspite of the minimum facilities like electricity, separate room, things are not attractive for the children.

At home also a few people are there, since most of the families are nuclear families. There is no elderly person to look after the children. On the other hand only a few one or two children in a family sometimes only one child in a family and the child is having single child syndrome. If both the parents are working they will meet only in the weekend sometimes once in a month. In this way the children do not get proper care by the parents. Thus the children are mostly deserted and diverted from the study.

As we have already entered in the 21$^{st}$ Century we need to take up this serious issues among the children's reading habits. Ultimately the children are the great loser in the cut-throat world market.

### Objectives of the Study

1. To investigate the reading habits of the rural children.
2. To find out the problems faced by the children, parents and teachers.
3. To access the situation and promote their reading habits.

### Hypothesis

- The rural children's reading habits drastically reduced due to the distraction by TV, Movies, Mobile and advertisements.
- The rural children are devoting veryless time for reading.
- The motivation is lacking among the rural children to increase their reading habits.
- The reading habits of rural girl's are significantly higher than the boys.

### Research Methodology

Research design : This study involved a survey of rural children in Dindigul District of Tamilnadu.

### Research Tools

A structured interview schedule has been prepared to obtain three types of information from the children, parents and teachers.

(a) Attitude towards reading habits of the children
(b) Problem faced by the parents
(c) Problem faced by the teachers

The scale used was the Five-Point Likert Scale

### Sampling Design

Simple random sampling was used to collect information from 200 rural children from two blocks in 10 villages. 100 parents and 20 teachers' one male and one female from 10 villages.

## Data Collection

The data was collected by using interview schedule from each child, parents and teacher.

Hypothesis were tested with a number of statistical analysis, cross tabulation, frequent counts, T-test, Reliability test and Factor analysis.

## Data Analysis

**Table 11.1: Educational Qualification of the Rural Children**

| Sl. No. | Name of the Villages | 0-5 Std. | 6-10 Std. | Above 10 Std. | Total |
|---|---|---|---|---|---|
| 1. | Thoppampatti | 6 | 10 | 4 | 20 |
| 2. | Chettyapatti | 2 | 12 | 6 | 20 |
| 3. | Anna Nagar | 5 | 8 | 7 | 20 |
| 4. | Kallupatti | 8 | 7 | 5 | 20 |
| 5. | Murthynayakanpatti | 7 | 9 | 4 | 20 |
| 6. | Mellkaraipudur | 5 | 10 | 5 | 20 |
| 7. | Oothupatti | 2 | 12 | 6 | 20 |
| 8. | Agaram | 10 | 6 | 4 | 20 |
| 9. | Mottampatti | 5 | 9 | 6 | 20 |
| 10. | Kollapatti | 4 | 10 | 6 | 20 |
| | **Total** | **54** | **93** | **53** | **200** |

The above table shows the educational qualification of the rural children. In this 54 children are studying 5$^{th}$ standard and 93 children are studying from 6$^{th}$ to 10$^{th}$ standard. 53 children are studying from 10$^{th}$ standard and above. Totally 200 children are taken from these villages. There is more number who are studying from 6$^{th}$ to 10$^{th}$ standard. It reveals that the enrolment is good and parents are sending their wards to school without fail.

**Table 11.2: Children's Reading Habits in the Class**

| Sl.No. | Name of the Villages | No. of Children | Percentage |
|---|---|---|---|
| 1. | Thoppampatti | 14 | 2.8 |
| 2. | Chettyapatti | 10 | 2.0 |
| 3. | Anna Nagar | 11 | 2.2 |
| 4. | Kallupatti | 8 | 1.6 |
| 5. | Murthynayakanpatti | 9 | 1.8 |
| 6. | Mellkaraipudur | 12 | 2.4 |
| 7. | Oothupatti | 14 | 2.8 |
| 8. | Agaram | 13 | 2.6 |
| 9. | Mottampatti | 12 | 2.4 |
| 10. | Kollapatti | 10 | 2.0 |
| | **Total** | **113** | **22.6** |

The above table reveals the number of children who are having reading habits in the class room. The reading habits are varying from place to place it is due to the backwardness of the village and the people who are having very less awareness about the importance of reading. Out of 20 children from each village the percentage is differing and in Kallupatti and Murthynayakanpatti village children are having less reading habits. It shows that children who are living in these villages are having very low motivation.

**Table 11.3: Children Reading Habits at Home**

| Sl.No. | Name of the Villages | No. of Children | Percentage |
|---|---|---|---|
| 1. | Thoppampatti | 10 | 2.0 |
| 2. | Chettyapatti | 8 | 1.6 |
| 3. | Anna Nagar | 6 | 1.4 |
| 4. | Kallupatti | 7 | 1.5 |
| 5. | Murthynayakanpatti | 6 | 1.4 |
| 6. | Mellkaraipudur | 8 | 1.6 |
| 7. | Oothupatti | 10 | 2.0 |
| 8. | Agaram | 9 | 1.8 |
| 9. | Mottampatti | 8 | 1.6 |
| 10. | Kollapatti | 10 | 2.0 |
| | **Total** | **82** | **16.8** |

The above table shows that out of 200 children only 82 children are having reading habits at home that is 16.8 per cent which is very low. Even in these 82 children the total children ranges from 6 to 10 in each village. From this we can understand that the reading habits of the rural children are not up to the mark. This is one of the very low profiles in the rural reality.

**Table 11.4: Children Reading Habits in Hours at Home**

| Sl. No. | Children's Reading Habits in Hours at Home | No. of Children | Percentage |
|---|---|---|---|
| 1. | One hour | 95 | 47.5 |
| 2. | Two hours | 80 | 30.0 |
| 3. | Three hours | 35 | 17.5 |
| 4. | Four hours | 10 | 5.0 |
| | **Total** | **200** | **100** |

The above table shows the reading habits of the rural children in hours. Out of 200 children 95 are having reading habits (47.5%) for one hour at home. 80 children are having reading habits for two hours that is 30 per cent. For three hours 35 children and for four hours only 10 children that is only 5 per cent. The more the hours the less the participation of the children. It shows that the reading habits are not very encouraging.

**Table 11.5: Children Reading Habits during Saturday and Sunday**

| Sl.No. | Name of the Villages | No. of Children | Percentage |
|---|---|---|---|
| 1. | Thoppampatti | 5 | 1.0 |
| 2. | Chettyapatti | 4 | 0.8 |
| 3. | Anna Nagar | – | – |
| 4. | Kallupatti | 2 | 0.4 |
| 5. | Murthynayakanpatti | – | – |
| 6. | Mellkaraipudur | 1 | 0.2 |
| 7. | Oothupatti | 2 | 0.4 |
| 8. | Agaram | 2 | 0.4 |
| 9. | Mottampatti | – | – |
| 10. | Kollapatti | 1 | 0.2 |
| | **Total** | **17** | **3.4** |

The above table shows the children reading habits during Saturday and Sunday. Out of 200 children only 17 children are having reading habits during Saturday and Sunday. More over it is not exceeding more than five children but in some places there was none. The total percentage is very low that is 3.4 per cent. If this is the reality how the rural children can develop the reading habits? A strategy has to be worked out for making them to read.

**Table 11.6: Children's Activities during Holidays**

| Sl.No. | Name of the Activities | No. of Children |
|---|---|---|
| 1. | Cricket | 80 |
| 2. | Play kabbadi | 40 |
| 3. | Play Thayam | 30 |
| 4. | Play Carom | 30 |
| 5. | Reading books | 10 |
| 6. | Reading news papers | 10 |
| | **Total** | **200** |

The above table shows the children activities during holidays. Out of six activities 80 children are playing cricket during holidays. 40 children are playing kabbadi during holidays. 30 children are playing thayam and carom during holidays. 10 children each are having habits of reading books and news papers.

Table 11.7 shows the educational qualification of the parents of rural children. In this 45 parents comes under illiterate category and 83 parents were educated up to 5$^{th}$ standard. 51 parents were qualified from 6$^{th}$ to 10$^{th}$ standard. 21 parents had studied from 10$^{th}$ standard and above. Still the illiterate parents are more compared to educated parents. Education up to 5$^{th}$ standard has been more but it is due to dropouts or they have discontinued from 5$^{th}$ standard to higher level.

**Table 11.7: Educational Qualification of the Parents of Rural Children**

| Sl. No. | Name of the Villages | No. of Illiterates | 0-5 Std. | 6-10 Std. | Above 10 Std. | Total |
|---|---|---|---|---|---|---|
| 1. | Thoppampatti | 8 | 8 | 3 | 1 | 20 |
| 2. | Chettyapatti | 8 | 8 | 2 | 2 | 20 |
| 3. | Anna Nagar | 8 | 7 | 4 | 1 | 20 |
| 4. | Kallupatti | 4 | 8 | 5 | 3 | 20 |
| 5. | Murthynayakanpatti | 2 | 9 | 4 | 5 | 20 |
| 6. | Mellkaraipudur | 5 | 8 | 6 | 1 | 20 |
| 7. | Oothupatti | 2 | 9 | 6 | 3 | 20 |
| 8. | Agaram | 3 | 9 | 7 | 1 | 20 |
| 9. | Mottampatti | 3 | 8 | 8 | 1 | 20 |
| 10. | Kollapatti | 2 | 9 | 6 | 3 | 20 |
| | **Total** | **45** | **83** | **51** | **21** | **200** |

**Table 11.8: Problem Faced by the Rural Children while Reading at Home**

| Sl.No. | Name of the Activities | No. of Children |
|---|---|---|
| 1. | No electricity | 40 |
| 2. | No proper place | 80 |
| 3. | A lot of disturbance | 40 |
| 4. | Family problems | 20 |
| 5. | Friends problems | 10 |
| 6. | Other problems | 10 |
| | **Total** | **200** |

The above table shows the problem faced by the rural children while reading at home. 40 children are not having electricity at home. 80 children are not having proper place to read. 40 children are having a lot of disturbance while reading at home. 20 children are having family problems at home while reading. 10 children are having friend's problems and another

10 children are having other problems. It shows that the present children wanted to read in a separate room without any disturbance.

**Table 11.9: Problem Faced by the Rural Children while Reading at School**

| Sl.No. | Name of the Activities | No. of Children |
|---|---|---|
| 1. | Teachers discourages to read other than subjects | 120 |
| 2. | Teachers compel them to read only subjects books | 160 |
| 3. | A lot of home work | 180 |
| 4. | Tuition teachers also expect the children to work very hard and complete the homework. | 190 |

The above table shows the problem faced by the rural children while reading at school. 120 children are having problems that the teachers are discouraging them while reading. 160 children are having problem with the teacher's compulsion.

**Table 11.10: A Lot of Psychological Problem Faced by the Rural Children while Reading at School and at Home**

| Sl.No. | Name of the Activities | No. of Children |
|---|---|---|
| 1. | One child syndrome | 160 |
| 2. | Shy to mingle with other children | 120 |
| 3. | Afraid to study | 180 |
| 4. | Poor children always try to be isolated | 140 |

The above table shows the psychological problem faced by the rural children while reading at school and at home.160 children were having one child syndrome and 120 children were feeling shy to mingle with other children. 180 children were afraid to study. 140 children were from poor background and felt always isolated. All these psychological problems have caused the children to behave differently.

**Table 11.11: Problem Faced by the Parents of Rural Children while Reading at Home**

| Sl.No. | Name of the Activities | No. of Children |
|---|---|---|
| 1. | Always watch TV. Not listen to parents | 40 |
| 2. | One child syndrome, parents feel afraid to make them to read/study well. | 20 |
| 3. | A lot of disturbance and distraction | 10 |
| 4. | Family problems | 5 |
| 5. | Other problems | 5 |
| | **Total** | **100** |

The above table revealed the problems faced by the parents of rural children while reading at home. 40 parents expressed that their children always watch T.V and do not listen to their parents. 20 parents were worried to make their children to make them to read/study because of one child syndrome and also the parents were afraid for children.10 parents expressed that they get a lot of disturbance and distraction while taking care of their children. Only 5 parents each are having problems in family and other problems. In rural area most of the family has only one child or two children. Even to take care of one or two it is a herculean task.

**Table 11.12: Problem Faced by the Teachers of Rural Children while Reading at Schools**

| Sl.No. | Name of the Activities | No. of Children |
|---|---|---|
| 1. | Not listen to teachers | 50 |
| 2. | Teachers feel afraid to make them to read/study well. They can scold or beat the children because their parents are very angry with the teachers if they beat their children. | 35 |
| 3. | A lot of disturbance and distraction | 15 |
| | **Total** | **100** |

The above table shows the problems faced by the teachers of rural children while reading at Schools. It is highly difficult for the teachers to control the children all the times. The children have more freedom than anybody else. In fact the teachers are very much conscious to cover the lessons.

At the same time the teachers are afraid to teach them through beating or stick. The teachers are facing a lot of problems in all sides like the Government gives a lot of work to be completed on time. The Head Master also plays a vital role to get good results. The whole education system is only marks oriented but not human oriented. Therefore, there is a need for innovative strategies to motivate the rural children to develop their inner personality and achieve their goals.

## Innovative Strategies

In order to achieve the goals of Central as well State government some innovative strategies are to be adopted.

- A number of rural children's library has been established with current books.
- Joyful learning and work based learning has been adopted in all villages and there was a tremendous support from the village children.
- Prepared talking books with the help of rural children
- News letters were prepared by the children to improve their knowledge and new ideas to explore their inner talents.
- Very small size books were purchased for them to develop their reading habits.
- Group reading practise was initiated
- Book review was conducted among the children.
- Drawing come workshop was conducted to commit them to prepare and spend their time in a creative way.
- Lending the books after reading it.
- The rural library was fully maintained by the children of these villages.

- The rural children know that they can compete the urban children.
- Parents meeting were conducted regularly.
- Teachers meeting were initiated and more number of parents and children participated in it. Various programmes were chalked out for the effective implementation of the library, and enhance the reading habits.
- Mobile library and exchange of books from one library to another was encouraged.
- Local news papers, magazines, journals have been prescribed for each library.
- Old books collection was done from the educated family.
- For the best performance award/prize was given to encourage them.
- Proper space and time has been fixed for the library.
- A lot of simple games were introduced.
- Establishing video conferencing facilities and interacting with the children to improve their language skills, mathematics and soft skills for the rural children.
- Involving local stakeholders for conducting the rural children library more effectively.
- Exchange of books through children to children makes a late of difference.

## Conclusion

Tremendous changes occurred among the rural children. These were possible because the participation was fully acknowledged by the team of dedicated staff and rural child leader. Now they secured more marks and self discipline has enormously developed. No one feels shy and isolated. They all participate in all programmes. For example last Gandhi Jayanthi was fully organised by the rural children. Children mobilized funds and invited the local panchayat leader and demonstrated to the other children in the village that it is possible for the children to organize it in a more successful manner. Thus, the rural institute is rendering and extending the service to the rural children for their total development.

## REFERENCES

Anderson. R.C. (1971) On Asking People Question About what they are Reading. In Arigatou Foundation, GNRC, (2008). Learning to Live Together An Intercultural Interfaith Programme for Ethics Education, Geneva.

Bower G.H. (Ed). The Psychology of Learning and Motivation (Vol. 9, pp. 90-132. New York.

Brown, A.L. (1982). Learning how to Learn from Reading. In J.A. Langer & M.T. Smith. Broke (Eds). Reader Meets Author/ Bridging the Gap (pp. 26-54). New York.

Chall, J.S. Jacobs, V.A. & Baldwin, L.E. (1990). The Reading Crisis. Why Poor Children Fall Behind. Cambridge. MA. Harvard University Press.

Karunakaran.T, (2006) New Constructive Programmes for Youth, Gandhigram Rural Institute, Gandhigram.

Raja. L, (2006). Kanavu Meipada Vendhum, Auspiration About the Rural Children, Department of Adult Continuing Education and Extension,Gandhigram Rural Institute, Gandhigram, India.

Raja. L, (2011). Need Assessment of the Children of Gandhigram Crèche Project, Department of Lifelong Learning, Gandhigram Rural Institute, Gandhigram, India.

Wilhelm, J. (2001) Think Alouds: Boost Reading Comprehension. Instructor. III (4) pp. 26-28.

# Education for 'US'

– A.Jahitha Begum

Education has been recognized as one of the cornerstones of India's development Goals as a strategy and its importance have been emphatically spelt out in the Indian Constitution. Reiterating this, the National Policy of Education 1986, resolved to provide free and compulsory education to all children up to the age of 14. A number of schemes and programmes have been launched in the pursuance of this foal. These efforts have led to considerable progress in terms of increase in institutions, teachers, and students in elementary education. *'Sarva Shikshaa Abhiyan'*, i.e. *'Education for All'* is the recent movement launched by our Indian Government with the objective of imparting Education for all the children in our country of the age of 14 within 2010. The goals and objectives of Education For All are:

Universal enrolment of all children, including girls and persons belonging to Scheduled Caste and Scheduled Tribes; Provision of primary school for all children within one kilometer of walking distance and of facility of non-formal education and Improvement of ratio of primary too upper primary school to at least 1:2. However the goal of Universalisation of Elementary Education (UEE) remains elusive. The elementary education it the country still faces several serious problems, including a large number of out-of school children, and low participation of girls, tribals, and other disadvantages groups.

One of the disadvantaged groups is the *NOMADS* or *MIGRATES* who are wandering form place to place due to many reasons. The prime and important reason is for their existence i.e. winning their daily bread. During my SSA supervision of the random checking of census work, I happened to visitor some of the disadvantaged groups. This made me to undertake this endeavour in 2001.

**Objective**

To identify the problems faced by the out of school children of the Migrates and suggesting remedies for their problems.

**The Sample**

The sample consists of the following places in the Coimbatore District.

A survey was conducted in the following places in the Coimbatore district. The list of the children given below did not attend the school so far irrespective of their age. The seven areas visited in the Coimbatore district itself consisted of nearly 46 non-going students, then what will be population of the out of school children of our State and also the whole nation? Moreover the aim of taking this project is to do the needful for these deprived children.

**1. Podanur Main Road**

| Name of the Children | Age | Name of the Parents | |
|---|---|---|---|
| 1. Vengatesh | 10 | Sinrasu | Ramakka |
| 2. Jegannadhan | 8 | Thiruppathy | Kuppu |

## 2. Kurichy Road, Sundaraburam, Ulavarsandai

| Name of the Children | Age | Name of the Parents | |
|---|---|---|---|
| 1. Appu | 8 | Akthar | Naseema |
| 2. Salma | 6 | Saube | Salma |
| 3. Salma | 8 | Akthar | Naseema |
| 4. Suban | 6 | Jaloo | Jareeena |
| 5. Sehinsha | 8 | Baseer | Subaida |
| 6. Sharif | 7 | Akthar | Naseema |
| 7. Reshma | 7 | Baseer | Subaida |
| 8. Thahir Hussain | 7 | Mammu | Farida |

## 3. Teachers' Colony, Sundaraburam

| Name of the Children | Age | Name of the Parents | |
|---|---|---|---|
| 1. Sabira | 12 | Hasan Ali | Sariba Beevi |
| 2. Samseer Hussain | 10 | Hasan Ali | Sariba Beevi |
| 3. Fatha Ali | 8 | Hasan Ali | Sariba Beevi |
| 4. Hyder Ali | 8 | Babu Ali | Punch Beebi |
| 5. Chandhini | 6 | Sara Banu | Raibal |
| 6. Appu | 7 | Jahir Hussain | Cheenu |
| 7. Noori | 6 | Hussain | Nouroon |
| 8. Najar | 9 | Nasar | Dhilloo |
| 9. Sabia | 6 | Nasar | Dhilloo |
| 10. Reshma | 6 | Gau | Jubaida |
| 11. Fakeeja | 7 | Hasanthagi | |
| 12. Mehandi | 7 | Gau | Jubaida |
| 13. Aslam | 12 | Husen | Nouroon |
| 14. Akram | 11 | Husen | Nouroon |
| 15. Javid | 6 | Jahangir | Jeenat |

## 4. Teachers' Colony, Sundaraburam

| Name of the Children | Age | Name of the Parents | |
|---|---|---|---|
| 1. Prasanth | 6 | Samikkannu | Santhi |
| 2. Gokulkumar | 7 | Samikkannu | Santhi |
| 3. Murugesan | 10 | Thnagaraj | Senamma |
| 4. Selvi | 11 | Thnagaraj | Senamma |
| 5. Eswaran | 6 | Thnagaraj | Senamma |
| 6. Sathya | 6 | Thnagaraj | Thnagaraj |
| 7. Sathya | 5 | Vadivel | Santhi |
| 8. Jeyasanthi | 12 | Veeram | Kuppammal |
| 9. Sathya | 6 | Medaiuappan | Malar |
| 10. Murugesan | 8 | Murugesan | Vennila |
| 11. Ravi | 12 | Iyanar | Selvi |
| 12. Manoharan | 10 | Govindan | Sinnapillai |
| 13. Jeyanadhan | 7 | Veran | Kamalam |
| 14. Savithri | 10 | Veran | Kamalam |
| 15. Sangeetha | 12 | Veran | Kamalam |

## 5. Chettipalayam Near Radio Station

| Name of the Children | Age | Name of the Parents | |
|---|---|---|---|
| 1. Pandian | 6 | Raju | Rojamallli |
| 2. Anjuponnu | 6 | Raju | Rojamallli |
| 3. Meena | 4 | Raju | Rojamallli |
| 4. Sakthivel | 9 | Natraju | Santhi |
| 5. Priya | 10 | Valpari | Surukkili |

Apart from the above five areas two more areas of Malumichampatti, Pollachi road were also visited. Nearly 10 families are residing here and at the time of my visit the children had gone to the nearby temple festival.

### Problems Faced by the Subjects

These deprived children could not have formal education because their parents are not staying permanently in a place.

Due to their occupational needs they have to 'shift' their 'residence' Moreover the parents do not have any time to think' about their children's education because winning daily bread is their only concern. They are not sending their wards to schools listed the following reasons.

1. As there are only formal schools, they could not send their children from June to April for one full academic year. Due to their job opportunists they could not stay in a permanent place form more than six months. The non-formal institutions are far away from their places.
2. The telephone line cable workers are staying usually away from the city, where school access is very difficult. The schools are situated atleast two kilometers from their tents.
3. Most of the parents are working on daily wages, they could not afford their children the necessary things.
4. Their children are also helping them in their work. The grown up children are staying and studying in their villages whereas the younger ones up to the age of 10 are staying with them without attending the schools.

I have visited only 7 areas of the Coimbatore district. The temporary households are of different types. They are.

1. Workers engaged in public works like cable work, their road workers etc.
2. The people called 'Narikkuravas'.
3. The migrants form Afghans who have settled in our country long back.

I have visited all the three types of temporary households. There are so many other types of peoples who are engaged in:

1. Toy making
2. Mirror work
3. Sheep rearing
4. Duck rearing and there are so many migrating groups.

These deprived children should be educated if the slogan of Education for all to be achieved. If adequate opportunities are provided most of these children will have a fair share of getting educated.

## Remedial Measures

The following remedial measures are given solve the educational problems of these deprived children.

### 1. Mobile Students

These children should be allowed to attend the nearby schools. They attend the schools as many days as they can stay in that particular area. An attendance certificate should be provided for those children so that with this certificate they should be allowed to attend the same class in the other school where they are moving next. In this way the children are getting the opportunity to attend the school continuously wherever they move along with their parents. As the syllabus is the same in the Government schools there won't be any difficulty in writing the exams also.

### 2. Mobile Schools

The Government, each school with one or two teachers, can set up mobile schools or 'Moving Schools'. These schools should move to the locality where these children are staying. In a day the Mobile Schools can visit two or three places so that the children of two or three areas can be benefited. In a district two to five mobile schools can be set up.

### 3. Children's Education Centres

Like Adult Education centers Children's Education Centers (CES) can be established for these deprived children. These children are socially, economically, culturally backward. The primary aim of these education centers should be primarily imparting the three 'r's and some hygienic guidelines.

# Say No to 'Child Labour' Say Yes to 'Education'

– Y. Bhaskaracharyulu
– Kapu Deepthi
– Y. Nirmala

## Introduction

The phrase *'Today's children are the citizens of tomorrow'* has lost its meaning, given the prevalence of child labour across the country. Child labour is a curse to our society and a crime against humanity. Children work when they are supposed to play or go to school. The sad thing is that they work under hazardous conditions. Though acute poverty is the main cause for child labour throughout the world, everybody - society, parents, government, individuals, low wages, unemployment, poor standard of living, deep social prejudices and backwardness are directly responsible for child labour in India.

The social scenarios, according to the Gurupada Swami Committee on child labour, have changed radically with the advent of industrialization and urbanization. Earlier, the children were employed in agriculture and plantation only, where they were involved in sowing, reaping, harvesting, thirsting etc, besides taking care of the cattle and toddler. But, industrialization has employed them in hazardous works like bidi rolling, fire cracker making, matchbox making, pencil making, bangle making, carpet making etc.

Child labour, although, is more prevalent in developing countries, it definitely a universal phenomenon. In Naples, millions of children are employed in leather industries. In Spain more than hundred thousand children work in orchards and plantations. An International Labour Organisation (ILO) study in the department of Madre de Dios has revealed that 20 per cent of the workers deployed in gold production units are from 11 years to 18 years of age. Thousands of children all over the Western World work in fast food centers, gas stations, newspaper selling, cleaning of cars and work in garment and leather factories.

According to the World Labour Report, the child labour is considered as 'forced labour' because children are rarely in a position to give free consent to any activities performed by them as most aspects of their lives are determined by adults. Though poverty forces families to send their children into labour, the employers find it a source of cheap and trouble-free labour. Children can be beaten and bullied into doing dirty jobs trade union take their responsibilities. Child labourers don't seem to have any rights.

What are the causes of child labour in India? How do governmental policies affect it? What role does education play in regard to child labour in India? The answers to these questions may lead us to possible solutions. This article discusses about the problems of child labour, how common it is and the types, the role of poverty and government policies. Education policies and their relationship to child labour are described. In addition, solutions to some aspects of this problem will be offered.

*"All the problems of the world- Child Labour and Corruption- are symptoms of a spiritual disease; lack of compassion."*

Causes of child labour are:

- Poverty
- Parental illiteracy
- Tradition of making the children to handle over their family working skills
- Absence of Universal compulsory primary education
- Social apathy and tolerance of child labour
- Ignorance of the parents about the adverse consequences of working
- Ineffective enforcement of the legal provisions pertaining to child labour
- Non-availability and non-accessibility of schools in rural areas
- Irrelevant and non-attractive school curriculum
- Employers prefer children as they constitute-cheap labour, not able to fight against exploitation, illiterate, they cannot organize into trade unions.

**Child Labour Legislation**

In India, however, there is no law which actually provided for elimination of child labour. The constitution in article - 25 states that no child below 14 years will be employed in factories or mines or engaged in any hazardous employment. But, nowhere does it make any mention of abolition or elimination of child labour. Although the Child labour Prohibition and Regulation Act of 1986 has suggested reasonable working conditions for children working in hazardous conditions. The term hazardous neither been clearly defined anywhere in the Constitution, nor in different legislation proposed on child labour. Thus, the interpretation of the term 'hazardous' is ambiguous and inadequate especially in the case of child labour.

The Government has sanctioned child labour projects in 63 districts in addition to 12 ongoing ones under the National Child Labour Project Scheme (NCLP). Under the scheme nearly 240 thousand children would be covered. Further, the government has also released Rs. 6.65 crore for district level awareness campaign to 133 most child labour endemic districts in the country. A detailed consultation with State Government and district officials from the most child labour endemic areas of the country has also been done. The government alone cannot deal such a great problem and a change in attitude is needed to eliminate/reduce this menace. If children of the poor can be provided education and vocational training and if stipends accompany such training, parents would be under less pressure to send their children to work in hazardous factories. But this requires a huge effort and a fresh thinking, which sadly is lacking and the blame for child labour must be shared by the society and the leaders.

**Constitutional Provisions on Child Labour**

The constitution is the law of land and any law framed contrary to it will be held unconstitutional and invalid. Our constitutional makers were about the problem of child labour, so they made prohibition of child in certain employment as a Fundamental Right under Article 24 and issued many Directive Principles of State Policies in part IV. Let us examine all constitutional provisions for eliminating child labour.

**Article 15(3)** - The State is empowered to make the special provisions relating to child, which will not be violate of Right to Equality.

**Article 21** - No person shall be deprived of his life or personal liberty, except according to procedure established by Law. The Supreme Court held that 'life' includes free from exploitation and to live a dignified life.

**Article 21A** - Right to Education - the State shall provide free and compulsory education to all children of the age of 6 to 14 year in such manner as the State, by law may determine.

**Article 23** - Trafficking in human beings and beggar and other similar forms of forced labour are prohibited and any contravention of this prohibition shall be an offence punishable in accordance with law.

**Article 24** - Prohibition of Employment of Children in factories etc.,- no child below the age 14 years shall be employed in work in any factory or mine or engaged any other hazardous employment.

**Article 39(e)** - The State shall in particular, direct its policy towards securing- that the health and strength of workers and the tender age of children are not abused and that citizens are not forced by economic necessity to enter avocations unsuited to their strength.

**Article 39(f)** - The State shall, in particular, direct its policy towards securing that children are given opportunities and facilities to develop in a healthy manner and in conditions of freedom and dignity; and that childhood and youth are protected against exploitation and against moral and material abandonment.

**Article 45** - The State shall endeavour to provide early childhood care and education for all children until they complete the age of six years.

**Article 51 A (e)** - It shall be the duty of every citizen of India, who is a parent or guardian to provide opportunities for education to his child or ward as the case may be, between the age of six and fourteen years.

*"children must be taught how to think, but not to do work"*

**Conventions on Child Labour**

*Minimum Age Convention 1973 (C138 of ILO)* – The International Labour Organisation established the Minimum Age Convention in the year 1973 and it was initiated for practice on the 19th of June 1976.157 countries have ratified this treat as of March 2011 with the latest being Cape Verde in February 2011.

Its main aim was to ensure the effective abolition of child labour and to increase the minimum age that children were permitted to be employed. It allows countries to decide their minimum age for employment for themselves with the lowest possible being 14 years. However, the convention permitted light work for children as young as 13 years old.

### Convention on the Rights of the Child

The Convention on the Rights of the Child (CRC) is a United Nations convention signed on 20th November 1989, and put into effect on 2nd September 1990. It sets out the civil, political, economic, social, health, and cultural rights of children. The convention defines a child as any human being under the age of 18 years, unless a country recognizes an earlier age of majority, and requires nations to act in the best interests of the child. The convention forbids capital punishment for children, obliges states to allow parents to exercise parental responsibilities, acknowledges the rights of children to express their opinions have those opinions heard and acted upon, protect children's privacy, protect from abuse and excessive interference. As an November 2009, 194 countries have ratified it.

### Worst Forms of Child Labour Convention

The Worst Forms of Child Labour Convention (ILO Convention 182) is a convention adopted by the International Labour Organisation on 17th June 1999, and put into force on 19th November 2000.

Among others, this convention contains recommendations on the types of hazards that should be considered for inclusion within a country-based definition of "Worst Form Hazards faced by Children at Work".

| Particulars | The Minimum Age At which Children can Start Work | Possible Exceptions for Developing Countries |
|---|---|---|
| Hazardous work.<br>Any work which is likely to jeopardize children's physical, mental or moral heath, safety or morals should not be done by anyone under the age of 18. | 18 years (16 under strict conditions) | 18 years (16 under strict conditions) |
| Basic Minimum Age.<br>The minimum age for work should not be below the age for finishing compulsory schooling, which is generally 15. | 15 years | 14 years |
| Light work.<br>Children between the ages of 13 and 15 years old may do light work, as long as it does not threaten their health and safety, or hinder their education or vocational orientation and training. | 13-15 years | 12-14 years |

## Child Labour Eradication Programmes:

The Indian government has undertaken programmes to eradicate all forms of child labour in hazardous and non-hazardous conditions and provided universal free primary education to the children. Not only the government, many of the NGO's are implementing many programmes to eradicate child labour and educate the parents about the importance of education. The following are some of such eradication programmes :

- International programme on the elimination of child labour (IPEC).
- Towards the elimination of the worst forms of child labour (TPEC)
- National Legal Research Development (NLRD).
- Society for Elimination of Rural Poverty (SERP) and District Poverty Initiatives Project (DPIP).
- Education Department and District Primary Education Programme (DPEP), Government of A.P.

## Child Rights

Child Rights are the Human Rights for children, which focuses more on special care and protection towards children. Child Right include the Right to associate with both biological parents, access to basic needs of food and water, education, and health care. The low social status afforded to children in most societies due to the fact children are not adults, subjects them to unfair treatment or being completely ignored in decision-making and other political topics. To overcome this issue, there are therefore a number of rights which apply particularly to children in the UN Convention on the Rights of the Child (CRC). These rights include the obligation to consider a child's views, and limitations on the use of children in an armed conflict.

Since the adoption of the CRC in 1989, it has been approved more quickly by more governments than any other human rights tool. The basic principle of the CRC is that children are born with fundamental freedoms and the inherent rights of all human beings. Further actions such as enacting legislations, creating mechanisms and putting into place a range of measures to ensure the protection and realization of the rights of those under the age of 18, has been put forward by many governments. The only two countries that have not ratified the CRC are Somalia and the United States, while many countries have also failed to enact the convention that they have signed to.

The following are some of the most violations of child rights and common problems faced by children are:

- Hazardous labour exploitation.
- Sexual violence and exploitation.
- Sexual abuse and trafficking.
- Recruitment as child soldiers.
- Physical abuse.
- Police abuse and arbitrary detention of street children.
- Orphans and abandoned children without adequate care.
- Refugees; children make up over half of the world's refugees.
- Lack of access to education or substandard education

The UNICEF Convention on the Rights of the Child (CRC), offers the following rights upon all the children across the world:

- The right to survival - to life, health, nutrition, name and nationality
- The right to development - to education, care, leisure, recreation
- The right to protection - from exploitation, abuse, neglect
- The right to participation - for expression, information, thought and religion

The Child Rights Information Network (CRIN) classifies Child Rights into two key categories:

- Economic, social, and cultural rights: This includes the necessary conditions to meet the most basic human needs such as food and water, shelter, education, health care, and beneficial employment.

- Environmental, cultural, and developmental rights: Which includes the right to live in safe and healthy environments, and that groups of people have the right to cultural, political, and economic development

## Parental Education

*"Education as an intervention strategy to eliminate and prevent child labour"*

Child Labour is a problem that is faced by the children. They get forced to work and are constrained from their own freedom of will. With no one to teach them their essential knowledge and treat them safely with dignity. They will grow up with thinking that the world owed them a living and will develop a dull, unhealthy or sometimes rogue mentality which will eventually make them lose their self-esteem, respect and forget their responsibilities as a human. They were not taught as how ordinary children should be taught i.e. that they have rights to their bodies, their feelings, their property, and to be treated by other with respect as a worthy human being. This will all ultimately point to one main cause which is; better parents.

As a child learning their basic essentials like health habit, manners, respect, etc. are needed, things that are usually taught by a parents or in a school which also would mostly require parents. Parents influence can arguably be the most important ingredient in a person's childhood. They are the only trusted source that an offspring can first look up to for guidance, advice and to be directed to the right path.

Therefore, in order to have the child labourers restored back to a classroom or have childhood life, there is the need of a parent, a parent who has the general knowledge one would require to raise children. For this the Government or even NGOs (Non-Governmental Organisations) can implement educational programmes or institutes that grant parents the knowledge they would need in life and to take care of their family and children. They could more specifically do it for parents of child workers, and who lacks the knowledge about Child Rights and the future consequences the child would face due to the hardships being faced at their young age. Through this education, the parents can learn about ways to overcome these problems and the requirements for them to succeed and pursue their goals. This can help the parents rehabilitate themselves and care for their children, ultimately reducing the number of child labourers.

It is also important of how the parents look after their child because sooner or later when the child grows up and needs to raise his/her own children they will remember how they were raised by their parents and thus the future of that child will be a result of how that child's parents were looked after during their young age and the lessons they have learnt during their growth.

*"Say no to child labour, and yes to education. . ."*

**Children Education**

The children at the age of going to school, to will go for work, for their family needs. Definitely they get exploited. The consumers buys the child labour, because they are illiterates, they are not aware of their rights, they can't demand the consumers for their benefits, they were not able to form a trade union, etc., everything is advantage to the buyer. After the parents, the children should be educated. The government can provide free education through establishing primary schools for between 6 to 14 years aged children. Many NGOs are organizing voluntary educational institutes and educating the children about the importance of education.

*"Education is the most powerful weapon which you can use to change the world"*

The following are some of the common figures of child labour around the world:

- There are 218 million child labourers in the world as of 2004, according to UNICEF.

- 14 per cent of all children between 5 and 17 years are child labours.
- 1 in every 7 children worldwide is a child labourer.
- 69 per cent of child labourers work in agriculture, hunting, forestry and fishing.
- Every year 22,000 children die in work related accidents.
- The proportion of girls working is not decreasing, and girls are more likely to be child labourers than boys.

But over the years progress had been made, from 2002 to 2006 the number of child labourers had decreased upto 11 per cent. And the number of children in hazardous work had decreased 26 per cent worldwide.

The following table describes about the identified and rehabilitated child labour in Andhra Pradesh.

| Zones | Identified | Rehabilitated |
|---|---|---|
| Visakhapatnam | 6098 | 5953 |
| Eluru | 7904 | 1495 |
| Guntur | 7078 | 628 |
| Kurnool | 5901 | 0 |
| Warangal | 2955 | 53 |
| Ranga reddy | 6108 | 5381 |
| Hyderabad | 577 | 264 |
| **Total** | **36,621** | **13,774** |

Action against child labour can be done by anyone. It can be Government, businesses, organisations, trade unions, consumers, normal individuals and even children themselves. The more activities done and interest shown on these issues the more the pressure increases on the use of child labour. Everyone should take responsibility in educating themselves as well as others, about these vindictive acts against children, and if everyone takes some kind of action the number of children workers around the world would substantially reduce, and the fight against child labour can result with success. Promoting education, adopting labour laws, educating and empowering the poor, improving codes of conduct, social responsibilities of business and the public and mobilizing society, etc. are some of the key initiatives that can and should be executed to have a good elimination strategy of child labour.

Any small action can help end the child labour issue, it might not seem much but that help is a great deal on the far side. It is better buying a t-shirt that just costs a little more in order know that it is safe and child labour-free than wearing one that used the blood, sweat, tears, or the freedom of a child. There will be enough people out there, who will be willing to pay to ensure that children don't suffer any exploitation anymore and that sacrifice can help save the lives of many children around the world, you could do the same.

If the Government do not support in the elimination of the exploitive use of children, it is the responsibility to act accordingly to fight against it. NGOs and the other movements can also pressure and urge governments to implement these laws, adopt its practice and support the fight against child labour.

**Consequences of Child Labour**

- Child labourers were deprived of their education, mental and physical development
- their childhood is stolen.
- Immature and inexperienced child labourers may be completely unaware of the short and long term risks involved in their work.
- Working long hours, child labourers are often denied a basic school education, normal social interaction, personal development and emotional support from their family.
- Beside these problems, children face many physical dangers - and death - from forced labour:
- Physical injuries and mutilations are caused by badly maintained machinery on farms and in factories, machete

accidents in plantations, and any number of hazards encountered in industries such as mining, ceramics and fireworks manufacture

- Pesticide poisoning is one of the biggest killers of child labourers. In Sri Lanka, pesticides kill more children than diphtheria, malaria, polio and tetanus combined. The global death toll each year from pesticides is supposed to be approximately 40'000
- Growth deficiency is prevalent among working children, who tend to be shorter and lighter than other children; these deficiencies also impact on their adult life
- Long-term health problems, such as respiratory disease, asbestosis and a variety of cancers, are common in countries where children are forced to work with dangerous chemicals
- HIV/AIDS and other sexually transmitted diseases are rife among the one million children forced into prostitution every year; pregnancy, drug addiction and mental illness are also common among child prostitutes
- Exhaustion and malnutrition are a result of underdeveloped children performing heavy manual labour, working long hours in unbearable conditions and not earning enough to feed themselves adequately

## Conclusion

Child Labour is a significant problem in India. Its prevalence is shown by child work participation rates which are higher in India than in other developing countries. The major cause of child labour is poverty. Even though children are paid less than adults are, whatever income they earn is of benefit to poor families. In addition to poverty, the lack of adequate and accessible sources of credit forces poor parents to use their children as bonded child labourers. Some parents also feel that a formal education is not useful, and that children learn work skills through working. Another cause is poor access to education. In some areas, education is not affordable, or is found to be inadequate. With no other alternatives, children inevitably spend their time working.

The Constitution of India clearly states that child labour is wrong and that measures should be taken to end it. The Government of India has set a minimum age of employment. This Act does not make all child labour illegal. Despite policies enforcement is a problem. If child labour is to be stopped in India, the Government and those responsible for enforcement need to start doing their jobs. Policies without enforcement are useless.

Education in India also needs to be improved. High illiteracy and dropout rates reflect the low quality of the educational system. Poverty plays a role in the ineffectiveness of the educational system. Dropout rates are high because children are forced to work in order to support their families. The attitudes of the parents also contribute to the lack of enrollment. Compulsory education may help in regard to these attitudes. The examples of Sri Lanka and Kerala show that compulsory education has worked in those areas. Hopefully the future will show that progress will be made towards universal education, and stopping child labour.

Child labour cannot be eliminated by focusing on one cause, for example education, or by strict enforcement of child labour laws. The government of India must ensure that the needs of the poor are filled before attacking child labour. If poverty is addressed, the need for child labour will automatically be reduced. Children grow up illiterate because they are working and not attending school. A cycle of poverty is formed and the need for child labour is constant from one generation to the next. India needs to deal with the underlying causes of child labour and the enforcement of laws. Only then will India succeed in the fight against child labour.

## REFERENCES

Bahara, D.S., Child Labour, Dimensions and Issues, Cyber The Publications, New Delhi, 2008.

Gopal Bhargava., Child Labour, Kalpaz Publications, Delhi, 2003.

Hugg D. Hindman., Child Labour, M.E. Sharpe, Inc., New York, 2002.

Nanjunda D.C., Child Labour and Human Rights, Kalpaz Publications, Delhi, 2008.

Parthasarathy K.. Child Labour : Socio Economic Context, Bharathidasan University, Tiruchirappali, 2007.

http://www.eclt.org/about-child-labour/child-labour-standards

http://labour.nic.in/content/division/child-labour.php

http://www.tnchildlabour.tn.gov.in/causes.htm

http://nchildlabour.info/HTML/Intro/CAUSES%20AND%20SOCIAL%20IMPACT%20OF%20CHILD%20LABOUR.htm

http://www.knowchildlabor.org/child_labor/consequences_of_child_labor.php

http://ncpcr.gov.in/Reports/Constitutional_Provisions_for_Child_Labour.pdf

http://nlrd.org/childs-rights-initiative/news-on-child-rights-violence-against-children/programmes-for-eradication-of-child-labour

http://www.ide.go.jp/English/Publish/Download/Jrp/pdf/135_7.pdf

# Teachers' Attitude Towards Inclusion of Children with Hearing Disability

– P. Renuka
– V. Jagadeeswari

*ABSTRACT*

The aim of this study was to survey the Attitude of school teachers towards the Inclusion of children with Hearing disability in general schools. For this purpose the investigator constructed an attitude scale, which consists of 45 items. The data were collected from 720 government school teachers of Chittoor District of Andhra Pradesh State. The statistical techniques such as Mean, Standard deviation, t-test and F-test were used to analyze the data. The results reveal that the teachers have less favourable attitude towards the inclusion of children with Hearing disability in general schools. However, the teachers belonging to different Independent variables (Except the teachers belonging to Independent variable –Professional status) showed no significant difference in their attitude towards inclusion of children with hearing disability in general schools.

## Introduction

A child with disability is one who deviates intellectually, physically, socially or emotionally so markedly from what is considered to be normal growth and development that he cannot receive maximum benefit from a regular school programme and requires a special class or supplementary instructions or services. The various categories of disability are - Hearing disability, Speech and language disability, Visual disability, Mental retardation, Learning disabilities, Orthopaedic disability, Giftedness etc.

Education of children with disabilities is a challenging field. Education generally enables a child with disability to overcome largely his disability and makes him into a useful child. The different types of available educational programmes for the children with disabilities are Segregated (Special) education, Integrated education and Inclusive education. Segregated education through special schools is very costly. So many educationists nullify the idea of Segregated education on the grounds that it never equalizes the educational opportunities; rather it creates a feeling of differentiation among children. Integrated education is an educational programme in which the children with disabilities attend classes with normal children on either part time or fulltime basis. Integrated education is less expensive when compared with special education.

Inclusive education has evolved as a movement to challenge exclusionary policies and practices of general schools. The principle of inclusive education is - all the children should learn together, wherever possible regardless of any difficulties or differences they may have. Inclusion is the full time placement of all children including the children with mild, moderate and severe disabilities in regular classrooms (Staub and Peck – 1995).

*Hearing Disability:* The Persons With Disabilities (PWD) Act-1995 defines hearing disability as loss of 60 decibels or more in better ear in the conversational range of frequencies.

*Attitude*: "An attitude is a dispositional readiness to respond to certain situations, persons or objects in a constant manner, which has been learned and has become one's typical mode of response"- Freeman

## Need of the Study

Now-a-days the education of children with disabilities is highly prioritized concern of both Central and State Governments. Favourable and positive attitude of teaches towards children with disabilities is a major and important aspect for the growth and development of children with disabilities in the Inclusive classrooms. In this context the researcher took interest in conducting the present study on "Teachers' Attitude towards Inclusion of Children With Hearing Disability in General Schools."

## Review of the Literature

Bird J., Bishop. D.V.M., Freeman. H. (1995) in their study on "phonological Impairments" compared the children with expressive phonological impairments with control children. Children with phonological impairments scored well below their controls on phonological awareness and literacy, independent of whether or not they had other language problems. Although many of them knew letter sounds, they were at reading and writing non-words as well as real words. The severity of the phonological problems in relation to age is an important determinant of literacy outcome, children who have severe expressive phonological impairments at the time they start school are at particular risk for reading and spelling problems.

Hoffman and Barbara, J. (1995) surveyed "Teacher Awareness of Speech and Language Therapists Roles and Services." The survey provided statistical results regarding the teachers' ability to recognize students – who had speech and language difficulties, teachers' knowledge of school based speech and language services and teachers' awareness of how to access the services of their students – who need them.

Mc Million, L., Bunning, K. and Pring, T. (2000) investigated "The Effectiveness of Deaf Awareness training course for support Worker of Adults with intellectual Disabilities Knowledge prior to the course was poor. Those attending the course significantly improved their knowledge and the use of strategies compared to a control group. Further research is needed to assess, whether gains made in training of this kind are transferred to the support of people with Intellectual disabilities.

Andrew, W., Smith, A. (2001) in their on "WHO activities for Prevention of Deafness and Hearing Impairment in Children" discussed the size of the problem and causes and consequences of deafness and hearing impairment. They emphasize an inadequate state of knowledge on this subject in the developing countries, described about the public health route for the prevention of deafness and hearing impairment especially through Primary Care and Health Centre and outlined the WHO aims and activities for prevention of deafness and hearing impairment.

Haward Jones, P.A, Whybrow J.J. and Sammers I.R. (2001) evolved simple electronic simulation of sensory neural hearing loss intended to raise the awareness of mainstream trainee teachers during role play as both teacher and hearing impaired pupils Trainee teachers experienced both roles during the simulation and their comments were scored by expert panel.

## Objectives

1. To examine the attitude of teachers towards inclusion of children with hearing disability in general schools with reference to Independent variables namely - Locality, Sex, Professional Status, Type of School, Age, Educational Qualifications and Years of Experience.
2. To find out the difference if any in the attitude of teachers towards inclusion of children with hearing disability in general schools with reference to Independent variables namely - Locality, Sex, Professional Status, Type of School, Age, Educational Qualifications and Years of Experience.

## Hypotheses

1. There exists significant difference in the attitude of Rural and Urban teachers towards inclusion of children with hearing disability in general schools.
2. There exists significant difference in the attitude of Male and Female teachers towards inclusion of children with hearing disability in general schools.
3. There exists significant difference in the attitude of Secondary Grade and School Assistant teachers towards inclusion of children with hearing disability in general schools.
4. There exists significant difference in the attitude of Primary, Upper Primary and High School teachers towards inclusion of children with hearing disability in general schools.
5. There exists significant difference in the attitude of four different Age group teachers towards inclusion of children with hearing disability in general schools.
6. There exists significant difference in the attitude of teachers with different Educational qualifications towards inclusion of children with hearing disability in general schools.
7. There exists significant difference in the attitude of teachers with different Years of experience towards inclusion of children with hearing disability in general schools.

## Sample of the Study

For the present study a total sample of 720 teachers working in government schools of Chittoor District of Andhra Pradesh State were selected randomly.

## Tool Used in the Study

The tool used in the study consists of 45 items with five graded options namely - 'Strongly Agree', 'Agree', 'Undecided', 'Disagree' and 'Strongly Disagree' having scores 5, 4, 3, 2 and 1 for positive statements and 1, 2, 3, 4 and 5 for negative statements. The responses of teachers were collected and corrected with the help of Scoring key.

## Statistical Techniques

The tabulation and analysis of data were done by using appropriate statistical techniques such as Mean, Standard Deviation, t-test and F-test etc.

## Analysis and Interpretation

**Table 14.1: Mean Scores of Attitude towards Inclusion of Children With Hearing Disability with Reference to Independent Variables**

| Sl. No. | Independent Variables | | Mean Attitude Scores towards Inclusion of CW-HD (Mid Point Value 135) |
|---|---|---|---|
| 1. | Locality | Rural (502) | 138.09 |
| | | Urban (218) | 141.01 |
| 2. | Sex | Male (408) | 139.77 |
| | | Female (312) | 137.94 |
| 3. | Professional status | SGT (533) | 137.83 |
| | | SA (187) | 142.24 |
| 4. | Type of school | Primary (398) | 137.67 |
| | | Upper Primary (130) | 139.22 |
| | | High School (192) | 141.52 |
| 5. | Age (In years) | 21-30 (81) | 141.78 |
| | | 31-40 (327) | 138.31 |
| | | 41-50 (216) | 139.43 |
| | | 51 & Above (96) | 137.86 |
| 6. | Educational qualifications | Inter D.Ed & below (109) | 139.26 |
| | | Deg D.Ed (99) | 140.26 |
| | | Deg B.Ed/M.Ed (302) | 138.83 |
| | | PG B.Ed/M.Ed & above (210) | 138.43 |
| 7. | Years of experience (In years) | Below 6 (117) | 140.36 |
| | | 7-13 (310) | 138.56 |
| | | 14-20 (165) | 139.09 |
| | | 21 & above (128) | 138.58 |

In the above table, all the mean attitude scores of teachers are not much higher than the Mid point value (135) and not nearer to Maximum value (225), hence it is concluded that irrespective of independent variables all the teachers possessed less favourable attitude towards the inclusion of children with hearing disability in general schools.

**Hypothesis - I**

"There exists significant difference in the attitude of Rural and Urban teachers towards inclusion of children with hearing disability in general schools."

**Table 14.2: Attitude of Teachers Towards Inclusion of Children with Hearing Disability with Reference to Locality**

| Sl.No | Locality | N | Mean | SD | t-value |
|---|---|---|---|---|---|
| 1. | Rural | 502 | 138.09 | 26.376 | -1.378 @ (p=0.169) |
| 2. | Urban | 218 | 141.01 | 25.622 | |

In the above table the t-value for the rural and urban teachers' attitude towards inclusion of children with hearing disability in general schools is not significant. It clearly states that rural and urban teachers do not differ significantly in their attitude towards inclusion of children with hearing disability in general schools. Hence the declarative hypothesis with regard to Locality is rejected.

**Hypothesis - II**

"There exists significant difference in the attitude of Male and Female teachers towards inclusion of children with hearing disability in general schools."

**Table 14.3: Attitude of Teachers Towards Inclusion of Children with Hearing Disability with Reference to Sex**

| Sl. No. | Sex | N | Mean | SD | t-value |
|---|---|---|---|---|---|
| 1. | Male | 408 | 139.77 | 25.223 | 0.930@ (p=0.353) |
| 2. | Female | 312 | 137.94 | 27.358 | |

In the above table the t-value for the male and female teachers' attitude towards inclusion of children with hearing disability in general schools is not significant. It clearly states that male and female teachers do not differ significantly in their attitude towards inclusion of children with hearing disability in general schools. Hence the declarative hypothesis with regard to Sex is rejected.

**Hypothesis - III**

"There exists significant difference in the attitude of Secondary Grade and School Assistant teachers towards inclusion of children with hearing disability in general schools."

**Table 14.4: Attitude of Teachers towards Inclusion of Children with Hearing Disability with Reference to Professional Status**

| Sl. No. | Professional Status | N | Mean | SD | t-value |
|---|---|---|---|---|---|
| 1. | SGT | 533 | 137.83 | 25.937 | -1.987* (p=0.047) |
| 2. | SA | 187 | 142.24 | 26.611 | |

In the above table the t-value for the Secondary Grade and School Assistant teachers' attitude towards inclusion of children with hearing disability in general schools is significant. It clearly states that Secondary Grade and School Assistant teachers differ significantly in their attitude towards inclusion of children with hearing disability in general schools. Hence the declarative hypothesis with regard to Professional status is accepted.

**Hypothesis - IV**

"There exists significant difference in the attitude of Primary, Upper Primary and High School teachers towards inclusion of children with hearing disability in general schools."

It is evident from the Table 14.5 that the F-value for the attitude of teachers working in Primary, Upper Primary and High Schools towards inclusion of children with hearing disability in general schools is not significant. Therefore it is stated that Primary, Upper Primary and High School teachers do not differ significantly in their attitude towards inclusion of children with hearing disability in general schools. Hence the declarative hypothesis with regard to Type of school is rejected.

**Table 14.5: Attitude of Teachers Towards Inclusion of Children with Hearing Disability with Reference to Type of School**

| Sl. No. | Type of School | Source of Variation | Sum of Squares | df | Mean Squares | F-value |
|---|---|---|---|---|---|---|
| 1. | PS | Between Groups | 1924.233 | 2 | 962.116 | 1.407@ (p=0.246) |
| 2. | UPS | | | | | |
| 3. | HS | Within Groups | 490380.366 | 717 | 683.934 | |

## Hypothesis - V

"There exists significant difference in the attitude of four different Age group teachers towards inclusion of children with hearing disability in general schools."

**Table 14.6: Attitude of Teachers Towards Inclusion of Children With Hearing Disability with Reference to Age**

| Sl. No. | Age Group | Source of Variation | Sum of Squares | df | Mean Squares | F-value |
|---|---|---|---|---|---|---|
| 1. | 21-30 | Between Groups | 944.576 | 3 | 314.865 | 0.459@ (p=0.711) |
| 2. | 31-40 | | | | | |
| 3. | 41-50 | Within Groups | 491360.002 | 716 | 686.257 | |
| 4. | 51 & above | | | | | |

It is evident from the above table that the F-value for the attitude of teachers with different Age groups towards inclusion of children with hearing disability in general schools is not significant. Therefore it is stated that the teachers with different Age groups do not differ significantly in their attitude towards inclusion of children with hearing disability in general schools. Hence the declarative hypothesis with regard to Age is rejected.

## Hypothesis -VI

"There exists significant difference in the attitude of teachers with different Educational qualifications towards inclusion of children with hearing disability in general schools."

**Table 14.7: Attitude of Teachers Towards Inclusion of Children with Hearing Disability with Reference to Educational Qualifications**

| Sl. No. | Educational Qualifications | Source of Variation | Sum of Squares | df | Mean Squares | F-value |
|---|---|---|---|---|---|---|
| 1. | Inter D.Ed & below | Between Groups | 241.469 | 3 | 80.490 | 0.117@ (p=0.950) |
| 2. | Deg D.Ed | | | | | |
| 3. | Deg B.Ed/M.Ed | Within Groups | 492063.129 | 716 | 687.239 | |
| 4. | PG B.Ed/ M.Ed & above | | | | | |

It is evident from the above table that the F-value for the attitude of teachers with different Educational qualifications towards inclusion of children with hearing disability in general schools is not significant. Therefore it is stated that the teachers with different Educational qualifications do not differ significantly in their attitude towards inclusion of children with hearing disability in general schools. Hence the declarative hypothesis with regard to Educational qualifications is rejected.

## Hypothesis -VII

"There exists significant difference in the attitude of teachers with different Years of experience towards inclusion of children with hearing disability in general schools."

It is evident from Table 14.8 that the F-value for the attitude of teachers with different Years of experience towards inclusion of children with hearing disability in general schools is not significant. Therefore it is stated that the teachers with different Years of experience do not differ significantly in their attitude towards inclusion of children with hearing disability in general schools. Hence the declarative hypothesis with regard to years of experience is rejected.

**Table 14.8: Attitude of Teachers Towards Inclusion of Children with Hearing Disability with Reference to Years of Experience**

| Sl. No. | Years of Experience | Source of Variation | Sum of Squares | df | Mean Squares | F-value |
|---|---|---|---|---|---|---|
| 1. | Below 6 | Between Groups | 300.366 | 3 | 100.122 | 0.146@ (p=0.932) |
| 2. | 7-13 | | | | | |
| 3. | 14-20 | Within Groups | 492004.233 | 716 | 687.157 | |
| 4. | 21 & above | | | | | |

## Major Findings of the Study

- There was no significant difference between rural and urban teachers.
- There was no significant difference between male and female teachers.
- There was significant difference between Secondary Grade and School Assistant teachers.
- There was no significant difference among the teachers working in Primary, Upper Primary and High Schools.
- There was no significant difference among teachers with different Age groups.
- There was no significant difference among teachers with different Educational qualifications.
- There was no significant difference among teachers with different Years of experience.

## Conclusion

In the present study the school teachers' attitude towards inclusion of children with hearing disability in general schools was less favourable. The teachers belonging to different Independent variables (Except the teachers belonging to Independent variable –Professional status) showed no significant difference in their attitude towards inclusion of children with hearing disability in general schools.

## Educational Implications

In the present study, the school teachers demonstrated less favourable attitude towards inclusion of children with hearing disability in general schools, which implies the need for the organisation of systematic awareness programmes on Hearing disability and workshops on the different methods of educating the children with hearing disability for the school teachers by the Specialists. Such programmes may develop more favourable attitude in the school teachers towards inclusion of children with hearing disability in general schools.

## REFERENCES

Amitav Misra, Dr. (2004), "Evaluation of Inclusive Education Practices and Implications for SSA in UP," Management of Inclusive Education, Seminar Report, p. 16.

Dash, M. (2000), "Education of Exceptional Children," Atlantic Publishers and Distributors, Delhi.

Janardan Prasad & Ravi Prakash (1996), "Education of Handicapped Children," Kanishka publishers, Distributors, New Delhi.

Vijayan, K. (2005), "Attitude of Teachers Towards Inclusive Education," Experiments in Education, Vol. XXXIII, No. 9, pp. 6-10.

# SECTION – III

## CHILD RIGHTS

# Rights of Children
## *Issues and Concerns*

– K. Devan
– S. Vidhyanathan

**Introduction**

According to United Nations Conventions on Rights of Child (1989), article 1 states "every Human under the age of 18 years defined as child". UNICEF (1946) estimated that 2.2 billion children are residing in the world among 7 billion world population with over 90 per cent of children are residing in the developing countries and one third of population are under 5 years of age (600 million).Like every humans children must be given equal rights but right from the history children have been abused, Harassed and suffering from homelessness, sexual abuses etc.

In the year 1776, Declaration of Independence proclaimed that "Life, Liberty and Pursuit of Happiness" as inalienable rights of Humans. Ratified this declaration, organisations like UNICEF, Children's Defense fund are conducting conferences and symposium, implementing goals for upliftment of children and also proclaiming rights for their advancement and betterment, irrespective of caste, creed, sex, race. Thus the subject "rights of child" hotly discussed in various parts of the world, but the participants are hardly children and the adults go on and on discussing the rights of child without the child actually getting any benefits from their lofty confabulations. Kofi Annan, UN former Secretary general rightly said:

> *"The idea of child rights then may be a beacon guiding the way to the future but it is also illuminating how many adults neglect their responsibilities towards children are too often the victims of the ugliest and most shameful activities" (September 2001).*

According to United Nation convention on rights of child (1989), an international body dedicated to the rights of child mentions that:

**Article1:** that the inherent right to life and the state's obligation to ensure the child survival and development.

**Article 24:** Health and health services: the right to the highest level of health possible and to access to health and medical services, with special emphasis on primarily and preventive healthcare, public health education and the diminution of infant mortality. The state's obligation of harmful traditional practices emphasis is laid on the need for international co-operation to ensure this right.

**Article 36:** Child labour: the state's obligation to protect children from engaging in work that constitutes a threat to their health, education or development, to set minimum ages for employment and to regulate conditions for employment.

As these rights shows that they are the fundamental rights of a child, but many nations seem fail to satisfy this. Particularly America and Somalia are the two countries yet not ratified with the conventions on rights of child (1989). America is the only country in the world are spending 711 billion dollars for their military expenditure, but not interested in the rights of child. Somalia, a country is being afflicted with civil wars. The situation in Somalia doubts the rights of children. Following records and data from international organisations has given the proof of nation's inefficiency to eradicate children's poverty and hunger. Because of poverty and hunger, children all over the world deprive education, starving and working as a bonded labour in various sectors for low wages, particularly in Asian and African countries.

International labour conference estimated 246 million child labourers in 2004, with 73 million under the age of 10 years; hundreds of thousands of children, especially boys participate either voluntarily or forcibly in armed conflicts as child soldiers. It is estimated that at any given time, there are 300,000 child soldiers under arm. The international labour organisation suggests that 8.4 million children boys and girls engage in prostuition, sex tourism and other forms of sexual exploitation. There are 250 million children between the ages of 5 and 14 years, for 120 millions of them work is a full time activity. Asia being the most densely populated region of the world consists of 61 per cent child labourers .32.5 per cent in Africa, and 7 per cent in Latin and Caribbean.

These data flashed the poor plight of children around the world especially Asian and African countries. Do these records show that they are having rights? Who has to blame? Moreover an incident in Somalia has shaken the roots of the child rights. A year before almost all the leading magazines flashed the photograph "A child and a vulture" in their front covers. That photo depicts that:

> *A little girl was crawling on the ground to reach feeding center and a vulture waiting for her. On the way to the feeding center she took some rest to regain energy and beginning her crawl again. This way she would reach feeding center after any days.*

Where are the human rights? Where are the child rights? This incident raises doubts whether there are any child rights. Many nations are saying that they are democratic and republic country, but they failed to satisfy the needs of child or rights of child. Do they think it is their rights? Every nation considered inanimate objects are sacred to their nations but nothing is sacred in this world rather than saving a child. Following words stresses this:

> *There is no trust more sacred than the one the world holds with children. There is no duty more important than ensuring that their rights are respected, that their welfare is protected, that their lives are free from fear and want and that they can grow up in peace.*
>
> *– Kofi Annan*

Proclaiming child rights and implanting conventions and declarations will not bring 100 per cent rights to a child. Due care has to be taken to uproot the evils which challenges the rights of child .A child when it comes as a citizen it has boundaries , but when it comes as a human it has no boundaries . If any nation failed to save a child, it will be a shameful act for all the humans.

## REFERENCES

Gopalakrishnan (2004), *Rights of Children*, Aaviskar Publishers and Distributors, Jaipur.

Alderson, Priscilla (2000), *Young Children's Rights*, Jessica Publishers, London and Philadelphia.

Mamata,T.,Sarada, D (2009) *Child Rights*, Discovery Publishing House Pvt Ltd., New Delhi.

Ness, Daniel, Farenga, J.stephen, Encyclopaedia *of Education and Human Development*, Pentagon Press, New Delhi, Vol. II, pp. 348-350.

Williams, Jane (2008), *Child Law for Social Work*, Sage Publications Ltd., London, California, New Delhi.

*The Invisible Soldiers: Child Combatants Centre for Defense Information*, Vol. XXVI, No. 4, July 1997.

http://WWW.globalissues.org/articles/82.

# Awareness of Child Rights

– R.S.S. Nehru
– Y. Bhaskaracharyulu

## Introduction

Human rights could be generally defined as those rights which are inherent in our nature and without which we cannot live as human beings. Human Rights and fundamental freedom allow us to develop fully and use our human qualities, intelligence, talents and consciences to satisfy the spiritual and other needs. They are based on mankind's increasing demand for a life in which the inherent dignity and worth of each human being will receive respect and protection. The first sentence of the Universal Declaration of Human Rights, states that *"Respect for the human rights and human dignity is the foundation of freedom, justice and peace in the world"*. Child Rights are part and parcel of Human Rights.

The world marks the 20$^{th}$ anniversary of the United Nations Convention on the Rights of the Child (CRC) on 20 November 2009; there is opportunity not only for celebration, but also for taking stock of the extent to which children's rights are respected and protected around the world. It is important that the educational policies that are developed in the best interests of the child, which enable the child to develop democratic values and human rights. Bearing in mind that, as indicated in the Declaration of the Rights of the Child "The child by reason of his physical and mental immaturity, needs special safeguards and care including appropriate legal protection, before as well as after birth"; Recalling the provisions of the Declaration on social and legal principles relating to the protection and welfare of children, with special Reference to Foster placement and Adoption, Nationally and Internationally, the United Nation's standard minimum Rules for the Administration of Juvenile justice (The Beijing Rules); and the Declaration on the protection of women and children in emergency and Armed conflicts.

The education service, though not having an investigative role to play in recognition and referral of abuse and suspected abuse, among all professional groups mentioned teachers have the role to play day to day sustained contact with children who can allow them to pick-up changes in behaviour, failure to develop and or other outward sign of abuse. Education welfare officers and educational psychologists also have a key role to play. All staff in education, related department should be aware of the need to alert social services and the police when they believe a child in or may be abused. Schools also have a role in prevention at child abuse through the curriculum with personal protection activities/programmes and parenting skills. The CRC is "the most complete statement of child rights ever made". It takes the ten principles of the 1959 Declaration of the Rights of the child, and expands them to 54 articles, of which 41 relate specifically to the rights of the children, covering almost every aspect of a child's life.

The need to make people aware of child rights concept is of paramount importance at this juncture. As a teacher educator the investigator witnessed many children suffering from different types of Vulnerabilities and the awareness about the child rights concept in teachers and parents. The investigator felt the dire need of inculcating the unawareness to the primary school teachers initially because teachers are the immediate responsible persons having concern about children. Teacher's role is very important in tackling the problems of children and protecting their rights. The present study is conducted on D.Ed Pre-service teachers to bring awareness on the rights of children also with a view that the child rights concept is equally important with other subjects.

**Review of Literature**

Swarnaprava Sahoo, (2002) "Development of a Curriculum Framework on Human Rights Education for the children below fourteen years of age" The study focuses on the basic human right issues concerning the in-school children and out of school children, below the age of 14 years with reference to their locality and sex. Also, an attempt has been made to develop a curriculum framework of human rights education adapted to the children below the age of 14 years. Survey Research Design was employed for Objective-1 and Case Study design for Objective-2. For objective-1 the samples for the study consist of 400 children, 200 parents, and 94 teachers drawn through quota sampling and incidental sampling techniques, respectively. An individual out-of-school child, selected for the study of human rights issues is considered as a case in this study. Six children - one each from urban slum boy, urban slum girl, rural boy, rural girl, tribal boy, and tribal girl were selected for the study. These children were selected on the bases of ease of access by the investigator.

Majority of the children belonging to tribal areas are deprived of their human right to health care, mainly due to poverty. Urban school children constitute the most advantaged with regard to enjoyment of right to health care, as compared to their counterparts belonging to urban slums, rural and tribal areas. Variation in the enjoyment of right to health care, between boys and girls has been found not significant across the localities. Poverty of parents, lack of awareness among the parents, distance between home and health center and negligence of teachers have been found some of the important factors often responsible for deprivation of school children from their right to health care. Due to unhygienic conditions in slums the slum children frequently suffer from anemia, skin diseases, and malaria fever. A majority of the tribal people prefer to consult Disari instead of doctor for all types of diseases. This has been attributed to distance of the health center from home and/or poverty. The school children of tribal areas and urban slums suffer more from economic exploitation as compared to their urban and rural counterparts.. Corporal punishment at home is a matter of concern for children belonging to urban slums. A majority of the tribal children have been reported to enjoy recreational and cultural rights more than the children in the urban area, urban slums and rural areas. In urban areas curricular pressures exerted by the parents and teachers, whereas, in rural areas and urban slums the pressures exerted by the poverty impede their recreational and cultural rights. The percentage of boys reported to enjoy this right has been found invariably higher than that of girls. Discrimination on the bases of gender, caste/ tribe or socio economic status of the parents has been found to have negligible existence in tribal areas. It is however a matter of great concern in urban areas, urban slums and rural areas. Education of tribal children, including girl child is not encouraged or supported by their parents despite interest of the children to pursue. Unemployment demotivates the parents in tribal areas to send their children to school. Tribal parents have been reported to favour education of boys more as compared to girls. There is however no gender discrimination in other aspects of life. Poverty is the main factor which deprives the tribal children of most of their basic human rights. Education of girl child is not encouraged in rural areas even in upper caste Brahmin families. A curriculum framework has been well designed on human rights education for the children below the age of 14 years.

### The Objectives of the Present Study

The objectives of the study can be stated as:

1. To find out the perceptions of students towards awareness of Child Rights.

2. To identify the significant difference between the opinions of boy and girl students towards awareness of Child Rights.
3. To identify the significant difference between the opinions of students based on their age towards awareness of Child Rights.
4. To identify the significant difference between the opinions of students based on their caste towards awareness of Child Rights.
5. To identify the significant difference between the opinions of students based on their religion towards awareness of Child Rights.
6. To identify the significant difference between the opinions of students based on their parental qualification towards awareness of Child Rights.
7. To identify the significant difference between the opinions of students based on their parental occupation towards awareness of Child Rights.
8. To identify the significant difference between the opinions of students based on their parental income towards awareness of Child Rights.
9. To identify the significant difference between the opinions of rural and urban area students towards awareness of Child Rights.

## Hypotheses of the Study

1. There will be no significant difference between the opinions of boy and girl students towards awareness of Child Rights.
2. There will be no significant difference between the opinions of students based on their age towards awareness of Child Rights.
3. There will be no significant difference between the opinions of students based on their caste towards awareness of Child Rights.

4. There will be no significant difference between the opinions of students based on their religion towards awareness of Child Rights.
5. There will be no significant difference between the opinions of students based on their parental qualification towards awareness of Child Rights.
6. There will be no significant difference between the opinions of students based on their parental occupation towards awareness of Child Rights.
7. There will be no significant difference between the opinions of students based on their parental income towards awareness of Child Rights.
8. There will be no significant difference between the opinions of rural and urban area students towards awareness of Child Rights.

## Methodology

Sampling is thus a study of the part of the different management schools in Visakhapatnam district. opinionnaire was constructed for the students to find out the awareness of Child Rights. The tool was prepared to find out the preliminary information about the awareness of child rights among students. Keeping in view the characteristics and guidelines for construction and also its advantages the investigator adopted the attitude scale and rating scale for finding out the opinions of students towards awareness child rights and for testing the hypothesis. For this study collect the data on this inference is drawn for the entire population. Sampling is thus a study of the part of the different management schools in Visakhapatnam district only.

The scholar adopted simple random sampling technique to identify the schools, students and students for collecting the data. Schools were selected on the basis of simple random sampling procedure. Students were selected based on the step wise simple random sampling technique. Altogether 20 secondary schools were randomly selected for the study.

A brief orientation is given before distributing the tool to the sample necessary instructions are provided to students.

No time limit is kept for the answering of the tool but almost all students answered the tool within half an hour time. Hence 100 students are selected from secondary schools in Visakhapatnam distract.

**Sample Distribution of Student's Category wise**

| Sl. No. | Variable | Category | No. of Students | Total |
|---|---|---|---|---|
| 1. | Gender | Boy | 59 | 100 |
| | | Girl | 41 | |
| | | 15 | 42 | |
| 2. | Age | 16 | 49 | 100 |
| | | 17 | 9 | |
| | | OC | 33 | |
| | | BC | 40 | |
| 3. | Caste | SC | 19 | 100 |
| | | ST | 8 | |
| | | Hindu | 64 | |
| 4. | Religion | Christian | 30 | 100 |
| | | Muslim | 6 | |
| 5. | | Illiterate | 31 | |
| 5. | Parental Qualification | Primary | 46 | 100 |
| | | Secondary | 22 | |
| | | Higher | 1 | |
| | | Labour | 19 | |
| 6. | Parental Occupation | Cultivation | 49 | 100 |
| | | Business | 19 | |
| | | Employ | 13 | |
| | | Below Rs. 25000 | 29 | |
| 7. | Parental Income | Rs. 25000 to 50000 | 69 | 100 |
| | | Above Rs. 50000 | 2 | |
| 8. | Locality | Rural | 7 | 100 |
| | | Urban | 93 | |

## Analysis of Data

As the present study is of more of qualitative in nature, collected data were analyzed using both qualitative and quantitative techniques. Quantitative data were analyzed with the simple statistical techniques. The investigation has been carried out by the descriptive statistical analysis, such as calculating measures of central tendency like Mean and calculating measures of dispersion like Standard Deviation. For testing the null hypothesis, the't' - test and Analysis of Variance have been used by the investigator. After the quantification of data, various statistical measures such as Means, Standard Deviations, 't' – Value and Analysis of Variance (ANOVA) have been calculated and presented.

## Interpretation of Data

**Table 16.1: Overall Perceptions of Students Towards Awareness of Child Rights**

| N | Min. | Max. | Mean | Mean Per cent | Std. Dev. |
|---|---|---|---|---|---|
| 100 | 32 | 160 | 146.64 | 91.65 | 3.80 |

From the above table students showed more positive response towards awareness of child rights. The mean, mean percentages, Standard Deviation are 146.64, 91.65 per cent and 3.80 respectively.

**Table 16.2: Comparison Between Boy and Girl Students Towards Awareness of Child Rights**

| Gender | N | Mean | Std. Dev. | t-value | df |
|---|---|---|---|---|---|
| Boy | 59 | 146.88 | 3.94 | 0.76 | 98 |
| Girl | 41 | 146.29 | 3.61 | | |

NS: Not Significant.

Table 16.2 observed that, the mean opinion scores of boy students with respect to awareness of child rights (146.88) is slightly higher than the mean score of girl students (146.29). The calculated value of't-value' is 0.76, which is not significant. This shows that there is no significant difference between boy and girl students respect to awareness of child rights. Hence, the null hypothesis is accepted.

**Table 16.3: Analysis of Variance (ANOVA) Perceptions of Students basing on their Age Towards Awareness of Child Rights**

| Age | N | Mean | Groups | Sum of Squares | df | Mean Square | F-value | p-value |
|---|---|---|---|---|---|---|---|---|
| 15 years | 42 | 147.48 | Between Groups | 52.42 | 2 | 26.21 | 1.84 | 0.16 |
| 16 years | 49 | 145.96 | Within Groups | 1380.62 | 97 | 14.23 | | |
| 17 years | 9 | 146.44 | Total | 1433.04 | 99 | | | |

NS: Not Significant.

Table 16.3 shows that, the ANOVA results of student's opinion with respect to awareness of child rights, basing on their age, between groups and within groups, the 'df' values are 2 and 97 respectively and sum of squares are 52.42 and 1380.62 and mean squares are 26.21 and 14.23 respectively. The F-ratio is 1.84 and the p-value is 0.16, which is not significant. Hence, the null hypothesis "There is no significant difference among the students basing on their age with respect to awareness of child rights" is accepted.

**Table 16.4: Analysis of Variance (ANOVA) Perceptions of Students basing on their Caste Towards Awareness of Child Rights**

| Caste | N | Mean | Groups | Sum of Squares | df | Mean Square | F-value | p-value |
|---|---|---|---|---|---|---|---|---|
| OC | 33 | 146.45 | Between Groups | 53.65 | 3 | 17.88 | 1.24 | 0.30 |
| BC | 40 | 147.03 | Within Groups | 1379.39 | 96 | 14.37 | | |
| SC | 19 | 145.47 | Total | 1433.04 | 99 | | | |
| ST | 8 | 148.25 | | | | | | |

NS: Not Significant

Table 16.4 shows that, the ANOVA results of student's opinion with respect to awareness of child rights, basing on their caste, between groups and within groups, the 'df' values are 3 and 96 respectively and sum of squares are 53.65 and 1379.39 and mean squares are 17.88 and 14.37 respectively. The F-ratio is 1.24 and the p-value is 0.30, which is not significant. Hence, the null hypothesis "There is no significant difference among the students basing on their caste with respect to awareness of child rights" is accepted.

**Table 16.5: Analysis of Variance (ANOVA) Perceptions of Students basing on their Religion Towards Awareness of Child Rights**

| Religion | N | Mean | Groups | Sum of Squares | df | Mean Square | F-value | p-value |
|---|---|---|---|---|---|---|---|---|
| Hindu | 64 | 147.03 | Between Groups | 29.90 | 2 | 14.95 | | |
| Christian | 30 | 146.07 | Within Groups | 1403.14 | 97 | 14.47 | 1.03 | 0.36 |
| Muslim | 6 | 145.33 | Total | 1433.04 | 99 | | | |

NS: Not Significant.

Table 16.5 shows that, the ANOVA results of student's opinion with respect to awareness of child rights, basing on their religion, between groups and within groups, the 'df' values are 2 and 97 respectively and sum of squares are 29.90 and 1403.14 and mean squares are 14.95 and 14.47 respectively. The F-ratio is 1.03 and the p-value is 0.36, which is not significant. Hence, the null hypothesis "There is no significant difference among the students basing on their religion with respect to awareness of child rights" is accepted.

Table 16.6 shows that, the ANOVA results of student's opinion with respect to awareness of child rights, basing on their parental qualification, between groups and within groups, the 'df' values are 3 and 96 respectively and sum of squares are 23.53 and 1409.51 and mean squares are 7.84 and 14.68 respectively. The F-ratio is 0.53 and the p-value is 0.66, which is not significant. Hence, the null hypothesis "There is no significant difference among the students basing on their parental qualification with respect to awareness of child rights" is accepted.

**Table 16.6: Analysis of Variance (ANOVA) Perceptions of Students basing on their Parental Qualification Towards Awareness of Child Rights**

| Parental Qualification | N | Mean | Groups | Sum of Squares | df | Mean Square | F-value | p-value |
|---|---|---|---|---|---|---|---|---|
| Illiterate | 31 | 146.90 | Between Groups | 23.53 | 3 | 7.84 | | |
| Primary | 46 | 146.43 | Within Groups | 1409.51 | 96 | 14.68 | 0.53 | 0.66 |
| Secondary | 22 | 146.50 | Total | 1433.04 | 99 | | | |
| Higher | 1 | 151.00 | | | | | | |

NS: Not Significant.

**Table 16.7: Analysis of Variance (ANOVA) Perceptions of Students basing on their Parental Occupation Towards Awareness of Child Rights**

| Parental Occupation | N | Mean | Groups | Sum of Squares | df | Mean Square | F-value | p-value |
|---|---|---|---|---|---|---|---|---|
| Labour | 19 | 145.79 | Between Groups | 36.23 | 3 | 12.08 | | |
| Cultivation | 49 | 147.18 | Within Groups | 1396.81 | 96 | 14.55 | 0.83 | 0.48 |
| Business | 19 | 146.00 | Total | 1433.04 | 99 | | | |
| Employ | 13 | 146.77 | | | | | | |

NS: Not Significant.

Table 16.7 shows that, the ANOVA results of student's opinion with respect to awareness of child rights, basing on their parental occupation, between groups and within groups, the 'df' values are 3 and 96 respectively and sum of squares are 36.23 and 1396.81 and mean squares are 12.08 and 14.55 respectively. The F-ratio is 0.83 and the p-value is 0.48, which is not significant. Hence, the null hypothesis "There is no significant difference among the students basing on their parental occupation with respect to awareness of child rights" is accepted.

**Table 16.8: Analysis of Variance (ANOVA) Perceptions of Students basing on their Parental Income Towards Awareness of Child Rights**

| Parental Income | N | Mean | Groups | Sum of Squares | df | Mean Square | F-value | p-value |
|---|---|---|---|---|---|---|---|---|
| Below Rs. 25000 | 29 | 145.83 | Between Groups | 29.13 | 2 | 14.57 | | |
| Rs. 25000 to 50000 | 69 | 146.94 | Within Groups | 1403.91 | 97 | 14.47 | 1.01 | 0.37 |
| Above Rs. 50000 | 2 | 148.00 | Total | 1433.04 | 99 | | | |

NS: Not Significant.

Table 16.8 shows that, the ANOVA results of students opinion with respect to awareness of child rights, basing on their parental income, between groups and within groups, the 'df' values are 2 and 97 respectively and sum of squares are 29.13 and 1403.91 and mean squares are 14.57 and 14.47 respectively. The F-ratio is 1.01 and the p-value is 0.37, which is not significant. Hence, the null hypothesis "There is no significant difference among the students basing on their parental income with respect to awareness of child rights" is accepted.

**Table 16.9: Comparison Between Rural and Urban Area Students Towards Awareness of Child Rights**

| Locality | N | Mean | Std. Dev. | t-value | df |
|---|---|---|---|---|---|
| Rural | 7 | 145.71 | 3.90 | 0.67 | 98 |
| Urban | 93 | 146.71 | 3.81 | | |

NS: Not Significant.

Table 16.9 observed that, the mean opinion scores of urban area students with respect to awareness of child rights (14671) is slightly higher than the mean score of rural area students (145.71). The calculated value of't-value' is 0.67, which is not significant. This shows that there is no significant difference between rural and urban area students respect to awareness of child rights. Hence, the null hypothesis is accepted.

## Major Findings

1. There is no significant difference between boy and girl students towards awareness of child rights.
2. There is no significant difference between 15, 16 and 17 years of age group students towards awareness of child rights.
3. There is no significant difference between OC, BC, SC and ST caste students towards awareness of child rights.
4. There is no significant difference between Hindu, Christian and Muslim students towards awareness of child rights.
5. There is no significant difference among students based on their parental qualification towards awareness of child rights.
6. There is no significant difference among students based on their parental occupation towards awareness of child rights.
7. There is no significant difference among students based on their parental income towards awareness of child rights.
8. There is no significant difference between rural and urban area students towards awareness of child rights.

## Conclusion

1. Students of Visakhapatnam district were showed more positive response towards the awareness of Child Rights.
2. Boy students expressed more opinion towards the awareness of Child Rights than that of Girl students.
3. 15 years age group students expressed more opinion towards the awareness of Child Rights than that of 16 and 17 years age group students.
4. ST caste students expressed more opinion towards the awareness of Child Rights than that of OC, BC and SC students.
5. Hindu students expressed more opinion towards the awareness of Child Rights than that of Christian and Muslim students.

6. Higher parental qualification students expressed more opinion towards the awareness of Child Rights than that of Illiterate, Primary and Secondary qualification parents students
7. Cultivation of parents students expressed more opinion towards the awareness of Child Rights than that of Labour, Business and employee parents students
8. Above Rs.50,000 parental income of students expressed more opinion towards the awareness of Child Rights than that of below Rs. 25000 and Rs. 25000 to 50000 students
9. Urban area students expressed more opinion towards the awareness of Child Rights than that of rural area students
10. The investigator, suggests the following topics for further study
    - The research work should be carried out on Child Labour Issues.
    - The research work should be carried out on other Class students in secondary schools.
    - The research work should be carried out on Intermediate and Degree level
    - The research work should be carried out on the implementation of Government provisions for Child Rights protection.
    - The research work should be carried out on the efforts NGOs in Child Rights protection.

## REFERENCES

Aruna Mohan Reader in education St. Joseph's College of Education, Guntur- Educational Psychological, pp. 38-43, Published by Lakshmi Naraayana Agarwal.

Bhagya Lakshmi L Lecturer, R.V.R.R. College of Education Guntur- Girls Education (Rurar Parents) Education Tracks October 2007, Vol. 7, No. 2.

Dash. B.N., Children's Right in Education Prospects. "Teacher and Education in the Emergency Indian society". Quarterly Review of Comparative Education Vol. 29. No. 2 June 1999.

Child Line, India Foundation Child Hope, UK. Department Women and Child Development, Government of India- Handbook as Child Line Protection Child Protection Manual pp 13-15 MHRD, 01 Annual Reports for 1986-87 to 2004-05.

Garret H.E- Statistics in Psychology and Education Bombay, Vakils, Fetter and Simmons Ltd. 1981.

Get Live advice from Keen ... Keen your Personal Advisor Over Phone on "Child Rights and Responsibility of Teachers" at Keen Government of India , 1974, - National Policy for Children, New Delhi: Government of India.

Indira Devi, P. Sr TGT, BHP & V. English Medium School, Vishakapatnam – Action Research Paper on "Effectiveness of Play-way Assisted Instructions Material to make Pupils Understand Child Rights.

Jagaiah C Lecture, RIE., Mysore – "Article on Challenges in Teaching Socially Disadvantaged Children" p. 6-14, Edutraks November 2003. Vl. 3, No. 3.

Kamalanayan Parmv Lecture. Shri R.P.Ananda College of Education Birgard, Gujarat - Action Research Paper in Early Children in Edutracks p. 32-33 April (2007) Vol. 6, No. 8.

Krishnamacharyulu V. Former Director SCERT, Hyderabad- "Educational Psychology". Elementary Education Vol. I and II.

Ministry of Education – Education Commission Report. 1964-66. Government of Indian, New Delhi.

Ministry of Health and Family Welfare – 2000, Annual Report, 1999-2000, Government of India; New Delhi.

Ministry of HRD, Government of India ... National Policy in Education 1982 and POA 1992.

Ministry of Women and Child Development, Government of India – Website www.wed.nic.in The Essential of Child Protection Handbook.

Mala Tandon, Department of Education North India Engineering College, Luknow – "Learning Disabilities Article Published in Edutracks July 2004 P 6-11, Vol. 3, No.11.

National Human Rights Commission – Annual Reports – 1993-94 to 2004-05.

NCERT, New Delhi – The Teacher and Education in the Emerging Indian Society.

Planning Commissions of India- Website www. Planning commission.

Savitha Bhakhrg – "Children in India and Their Rights" National Human Rights Commission, New Delhi.

URIE BRONFEN BRENHER- Ecological Systems Theory, pp: 1-5.

UNICEF Innocenti Research Centre- 2006, Website www.unicef.org/research for the 'Compilation of General Comments the Committee on the Rights of the Child'.

UNICEF – 2002, A World Fit for Children, New Delhi: UNICEF.

United Nations – 1989, Convention on the Rights of the Child.

United Nations Wbsite-www.unhchr.ch/html/menu5/child 90.htm for the Declaration and Plan of Action Adopted at the World Summit for Children, 1990-1998, UN Briefing Papers – Human Rights Today: A united Nations priority, New York. Department of Public Information United Nations.

Vanajam., Lecture; Guntur – A/ConF. 157/23, 12 July 1993. (Website: www.unhchr.ch/huridoctta/huridoca.nst).

Vienna Declaration and Programme of Action- Context and Constructs of Human Rights Education p. 6-14 Edu Tracks Nov. 2003, Vol. 3, No. 3.

## Important Websites

www.nhrc.nic.in (National Human Rights Commission)

www.wcd.nic.in (Ministry of women and Child Development)

www.socialjustice.nic.in (Ministry of Social Juice and empowerment)

www.mohfw.nic.in (Ministry of Health and Family welfare)

www.education.nic.in (Department of school Education & Literacy and Department of Higher education)

www.lawmin.nic.in (Ministry of Law and Justice)

www.planningcommission.gov.in (Planning Commission of India)

www.unicef.org (UNICEF)

www.un.org (United Nations)

www.ohchr.org. (UN.High Commissioner for Human Rights.)

# Status of Child Rights in India
## *A Critical Appraisal*

– C. Jim Jesudoss

### Introduction

Today India's Child population is 44 per cent (population census 2010) where as direct budget allocations are made only for 5.3 per cent. Here remains the contradiction which is reflected in every sphere of the society. Millions of Children in India go unnoticed and their participation is totally denied. The mere status of 'recipients' make them invisible in the large structures of the society. Their participation in governance remains a utopian concept for the adult world. But for children it is a reality and their willingness to participate remains unshattered. Children have the potential to contribute to the plan and design of policies and programmes aiming at their holistic development and the development of the society to a larger extent. The concept of Child Rights is anew to the Indian culture which gives much focus to communities rather than individuals. Children are part of any society or community where their presence is significant in the operation of the society either directly or indirectly. Thus, this paper attempts to make an historical appraisal of the status of child rights in India.

**What is Right?**

The term 'Right' is the most misunderstood word because of its abstract nature. Common man is always put in a dilemma, whether it is wants or needs. To have a simple understanding of 'Right' can be defined as 'those basic needs of every living being which are necessary for its existence". Yes 'Right' is only for living beings and it has a very close connection to life's existence. Take a tree for instance; It needs soil, water, sunlight, air and protection from danger. Every basic need is a 'Right' and removal of any one of those rights will lead to the death of the tree. These basic rights are inalienable and non negotiable. Every right is equally important for its living and healthy growth.

**What are Human Rights?**

Human beings are also living beings, but they cannot just live with the basic needs. Yes the basic needs are important for life's existence but for to have a dignified life and to have opportunities for growth the rights spectrum expands for human beings to a wider horizon.

Human rights can be defined as "Human Rights are the rights and freedoms that everybody had from the moment of conception, simply because they are human beings. Human Rights would ensure self dignity and self respect of all human beings". Thus the dignity and self respect of every human being is important and even the provision of basic needs should be made with due consideration to the dignity of every human being.

**What is Child Rights?**

Every child is a human being. The popular quotation says that 'child is the father of man' which is true that every child has his or her own self esteem and individuality. In simple terms one can say that human rights of children are called child rights. Many rights coming under the purview of human rights are the same for child rights too. There are few major differences between human rights and child rights. The Right to work, Right to marriage and Right to vote are a few exclusive rights for adults where as Right to play and Right to parental care are some rights pertaining only to children. There are many rights common for both children and adults. The civil rights including choosing one's own religion is common for adults and children.

## History of Child Rights

Every child born into this world cries immediately and makes her or his presence known to the people around her or him. Every child demands his or her rights from the immediate care givers. Though the history of child rights begins time immemorial for our understanding we can look at the recent past. The history of child rights in the modern era begins with the World War I. The world war was fought between 1914 and 1918. Children were the most affected among the war victims. Many children lost their parents and left in institutional care. In 1919 the world congress on Human Rights was formed. In the year 1923, Ms.Eglantine Jebb, the founder of Save the Children Fund brought a five point declaration emphasizing on children's rights. This gained greater attention from the international community which led to the emergence of the 'declaration on child rights'.

While there were considerable amount of efforts put in to ensure the implementation of this declaration unfortunately the World War II erupted between 1939 and 1945. Adolf Hitler emerged as the leader of Germany which led to the biggest carnage of people in the human history. Again the children of the world were got affected by the war and its aftermath. At the end of World War II the world leaders came together and founded the United National Organisations in 1945 to ensure peace and co-operation among the countries of the world.

Through sustained efforts the Universal Declaration of Human Rights (UDHR) was brought by the UNO in 1948.

Even in the UDHR there were not much significance given to children's rights which brought dissatisfaction among the child rights advocates across countries. It took three decades for the UNO to announce 1979 as the year of the child. This brought 'child rights' again to the center stage and lot of interest was developed among member states. This also led to continued lobbying and advocacy within and outside UNO to bring a separate treaty focusing exclusively on children's rights.

**Convention on the Rights of the Child**

In the year 1989 on 20th November the Convention on the Rights of the Child was passed by the general assembly of UNO which has become a milestone in the history of child rights. The dream that Eglantine Jebb developed for the children of the world has become true on that day. She is known as the mother of UNCRC. The convention on the Rights of the Child which is also known as UNCRC gives a larger frame work for child rights which could be expanded to every cultural context. It is the first legally binding instrument designed to protect and promote the rights of people under 18 years old. The UNCRC is the only UN document which is closer to ratification. It has 54 articles which covers a wide range of rights pertaining to children. It also gives clear mandate and guidance to governments for the effective implementation of UNCRC.

The rights of children can be classified into five major categories.

- Right to Provision
- Right to Life
- Right to Development
- Right to Development and
- Right to Participation.

**India Signed and Ratified**

On 11th December 1992 India ratified the UNCRC and has become a signatory to this convention and committed for its implementation. This has brought radical changes in the development sector changing the charity approach to the rights based approach. The UNCRC is the only document given authentication to the civil and political rights of children which has changed the equations. The adults including the government has become 'duty bearers' and the children have become 'right holders'. The rights based approach empowers children for being part of any decisions affecting children.

### The Status of Child Rights in India

India being a signatory to the United Nations Convention on the Rights of the Child (UNCRC) it is expected to play a proactive role in providing and protecting every right of its child citizens. Unfortunately for innumerous reasons most of India's children live in vulnerable situations leading to exploitation and abuse of children at a tender age. Children are robed of their childhood and forced to live in extremely unsafe conditions. The following alarming statistics explains it vividly.

- Less than half of India's children between the age 6 and 14 go to school.
- A little over one-third of all children who enroll in grade one reach grade eight.
- At least 35 million children aged 6 - 14 years do not attend school.
- 53 per cent of girls in the age group of 5 to 9 years are illiterate.
- High cost of private education need to work to support their families and little interest in studies are the reasons given by 3 in every four drop-outs as the reason they leave.
- Dropout rates increase alarmingly in class III to V, its 50 per cent for boys, 58 per cent for girls.
- More than 50 per cent of girls fail to enroll in school; those that do are likely to drop out by the age of 12.

**Conspiracy 1: Who is a Child?**

The UNCRC defines a child as "a person below the age of eighteen". Though India is a signatory still many Indian legislatures defines the child differently. The Child Labour Regulation and Prohibition Act defines a child as a person below 14 years; The Prevention of Sexual offenses against children Act stops at 16 years; the pediatric Act covers children upto 12 years and so on. The recent 'Right to Education Act 2009 defines children as persons between the age of 6 and 14 years. Defining a child differently in different acts actually denies the legal status of a child and many children go missing without any notice. Denial of a legal status leads to denial of basic rights to children. Children between the age of 14 and 18 are in their prime age and ensuring their rights is crucial for the present and future of our country.

**Conspiracy 2: India has not ratified article 32**

It is unfortunate that till date India has not ratified article 28 which exclusively focuses of the issue of Child Labour. This leads to millions of children dropping out from school and joining the labour force at tender ages. Though there are fragmented efforts made by the government to eradicate child labour the major setback is non ratification of this article. It is right time that India ratified this article and ensures quality education to all its child citizens.

**Conspiracy 3: Denial of Right to Participation**

The best interest of the child is one of the few major guiding principles of UNCRC. But when it comes to civil and political rights of children this principle goes against children. The duty bearers either the government or the parents think that they can do everything on behalf of the child which denies the participation of children in the decision making process concerning children's rights.

*"State Parties shall assure to the child, who is capable of forming his or her own views, the right to express those views freely in all matters affecting the child, the views of the child being given due weight in accordance with the age and maturity of the child."* Article

12 of the United Nations Convention on the Rights of the Child (UNCRC) is totally neglected by parents, teachers, community leaders and government officials.

**Suggestions to improve the status of child rights in India:**

1. **Promoting Child Rights**
   - To uphold the rights of rural children
   - To provide child rights education through participatory learning methods.
   - To educate the stake holders on Child Rights and enable them to become active promoters of children's rights.
2. **Holistic Development of Children**
   - To promote enhanced access to the school system and prevent children from dropping out of school to work
   - To identify and motivate children out of school and find placement for them in schools
   - To provide meaningful recreation for rural children
   - To offer counseling and guidance to children who need special care
   - To develop children's personalities through group activities and children's camps
   - To promote education and vocational training
3. **Ensure Protection of children**
   - To animate Community based organisations such as Self Help Groups, farmers group, local schools, panchayats on child protection
   - Through community participation advocate for issues affecting children and ensure children's voices being heard.
   - To facilitate the participatory process of developing child protection standards for each panchayat and enable them to adhere to those standards.

### 4. Promote Children's Participation

- To organise children of each village or urban habitat into Children forums and facilitate leadership development through democratic processes.
- To federate the base groups into cluster level/ district level/state level net work for advocacy and facilitate children formulate their advocacy agenda.
- To enable children to access appropriate information for their development.
- To enable children and their representatives to participate in decision making in matters concerning their rights.
- To enable children to participate in governance at the village/area level.

## Conclusion

When we look at the implementation of child rights India has done much but still it's a long way to go. Even among the Indian states there are much differences. Building awareness on Child Rights would definitely bring radical changes in the approaches of schools. Child Rights education could be part of teacher education and school curriculum which would enhance the perspectives of children and adults in ensuring children's rights. Including children in the governance processes is also a must which should be made mandatory for the elected governments to listen to children. The vision of Every Right for Every Child would be realized only through collective sustained efforts of civil society groups and government in partnership with children.

## REFERENCES

Abolition of Child Labour in India - Strategies for the Eleventh Five Year Plan: Submitted by National Commission for Protection of Child Rights to Planning Commission, India.

Budget for Children: India's Financial Commitment to the Child. HAQ Centre for Child Rights.

Child Rights in India: Current Status and Challenges.

Children in India and Their Rights Dr. Savita Bhakhri, National Human Rights Commission.

Every Right for Every Child 2003.

HAQ's Submission to the 13th Session of the Universal Periodic Review.

Ministry of Women and Child Development.

National Plan of Action for Children, 2005.

National Child Labour Policy, 1987.

National Policy on Education.

National Child Labour Policy for Children.

The United Nations Convention on the Rights of the Child November 20, 1989.

World Fit for Children, 2002.

WHO Child Growth Standards 2006.

7th All India Education Survey, 2002.

# Rights of an Indian Child
## *With Special Reference to Juveniles*

– C.Gayatri Devi

## Introduction

Children, the future assets of a nation have to be protected and must be given every opportunity to receive education, gain knowledge of men and materials and blossom in such an atmosphere that on reaching adulthood, must become a person with a mission and one who matters positively for the society. Although, infancy and childhood occupy only a fraction of the lifespan, they are the most crucial formative years in determining and influencing the personality of the adulthood. Hence, law and legal systems are expected to protect them from abuse of authorities either at home, or at schools, or at systems of administration of justice duly considering their tender age, incapacity to understand things in the perspective of worldly knowledge.

"The child by reason of his physical and mental immaturity needs special safeguards and care including appropriate legal protection before as well as after birth"[1]. A human child means any human being below the age of

18 years unless under the law applicable to the child, majority is attained earlier[2]. This definition of child, given by the International Convention, allows individual countries to determine, according to their own discretion, the age limit of a child in accordance with their own laws. The Census of India considers children to be any person below the age of 14 years for the purpose of government programmes. Indian legislations relating to children also define children in different age limits. For example, the Indian Penal Code 1860 categorized children as below 7 years, below 12 years, below 16 years and below 18 years for punishing them for various offences. Indian Constitution Article 21-A considered child as being below 14 years as child and State has to provide free and compulsory education to the children between the age group of 6-14. Factories Act 1948 defines a child as of below 14 years. For prohibition of child marriages and for adoption, the legislations mentioned different age limits. Even though the Juvenile Justice Act 1986 defined a boy child as below 16 years and a girl child as below 18 years, the 2000 Amendment removes this discrimination and a child means an individual below 18 years whether it is a boy or girl. According to the UNICEF records, such children in our country are more than 37.83 per cent i.e., around 440 millions of the total population.

## Historical Background

The beginning of the movement for the rights of the child can be traced back to the mid-nineteenth century with the publication of an article in June 1852 by Slagvolk titled "The Rights of Children" followed by Kate Kliggins " Children's Rights " in 1892[3]. With the attention gradually shifting to the working conditions of children, the legal position of children began to change with the introduction of factory laws which concentrated on the amelioration of the working conditions of employees especially children[4].

## International Concern

The first impression of international touch over the situation of children came in 1923 when the council of the newly established non-governmental organisation "Save the Children International Union' adopted a five point declaration on the rights of the child. In 1924, the fifth Assembly of the League of Nations endorsed this Geneva declaration and in 1948, the Geneva Assembly of the United Nations approved it. In 1951, a new Declaration for the welfare and protection of child was adopted.

The convention on the Rights of the Child 1989 marked the culmination of the efforts to bring the international community to recognize the needs of the children[5]. This Convention imposes a duty on the States to undertake all appropriate legislative, administrative and other measures for the implementation of the rights recognized in it[6]. Rio Declaration of 1992 and World Conference on Human Rights 1993 also reiterated and ratified the principle mentioned in this Convention and gave more and more importance to the rights of the child. The International Covenant on Civil and Political Rights (ICCPR) also states that the child has to be protected and rights are to be provided irrespective of his origin, religion, caste etc[7].

**Indian Constitutional Rights**

The Constitution of India, it may be said, is solicitous of the children's wellbeing, development and their rights in that when it speaks about children, it speaks about all children of the country, irrespective of birth, faith, caste, creed or sex. Our Constitution provides number of provisions for the welfare of children starting with Preamble. It promises to secure to all citizens of India (citizens include children also) justice – social, economic and political and liberty – of thought, expression, belief of faith and worship. The Constitution further provides equality of status and of equal opportunity under Art.14, and assures dignity to the individual under Art.21[8]. Art 15(3) enables the State to make special provisions for children. Art. 23 prohibits trafficking of human being and forced labour. Art.24 prohibits employment of children below the age of 14 years in factories, mines or any other hazardous occupations. Art. 38 enjoins the State to secure a social order for the promotion of welfare of people and people includes children. Art. 39 (e & f) directs the State to ensure that children are given opportunities and facilities to develop in a healthy manner and in conditions of freedom and dignity and that the childhood and youth are protected against exploitation and against moral and material abandonment. Art.45 states that State shall endeavor to provide early childhood care and education for all children until they complete the age of six years. Art. 21–A, added in 2002, directs the State to provide free and compulsory education to the children between the age of 6-14 years[9].

**National Policy**

National Policy Resolution for Children was formulated in the year 1974 and National Children's Board was constituted in the year 1975 with the Prime Minister as its president. The main objectives of creating the Board was to bring about greater awareness and promote the welfare of children and to plan, review and co-ordinate programmes and services directed at children. Some of the measures of this National Policy which was approved by Parliament in May 1986 are:

- State shall take steps to provide free and compulsory education for all children up to the age of 14 years.
- To provide informal education to those children who are not able to take advantage of formal education. To implement this, the Central Government launched "Sarva Siksha Abhiyan" to the children of habitants where there were no schools, to the working children, to the children of scheduled tribes and to girls who could not attend whole-day school. Agencies such as non-profit , public trusts and registered societies were given grant-in-aid by the Grant-in-Aid Committee appointed by the Ministry of Human Resources Development for carrying out "Educational Innovation" projects[10]. The very purpose of the non-formal education policy was that the children

not fortunate enough to be able to attend schools during usual school hours, or access a school, would still be made functionally literate and eventually get absorbed into the formal system[11].

- Protection against neglect, cruelty and exploitation.
- Below 14 years child shall not be employed in hazardous occupations and
- Existing laws should be amended so that in all legal disputes, the interests of children are given paramount consideration.

## Other Legislations

### 1. The Right of Children to Free and Compulsory Education Act, 2009:

According to this Act, free education has to be provided to the children within the age group of 6-14 years by the State and this Act is applicable to all 'recognized' schools. To run a school, recognition is mandatory and it will be granted if the school fulfills certain norms and standards prescribed in the Schedule of the Act. The conditions are include possession of an all-weather building with separate toilets for boys and girls, a kitchen, playground, play materials, games and sports equipment and a library with news papers, magazines etc. The consequences of running a school without such recognition are a fine of up to one lakh rupees and Rs.10,000 per each day as long as the contravention continues. In other words, a school without these facilities will not be allowed to function and will be prohibited. Hence, all the schools come under the purview of this legislation and all the school children's rights will be protected. This legislation provides for 25 per cent reservation for children belonging to the weaker and disadvantaged sections of the society in private and unaided schools also whereas such reservations were available earlier in government and aided schools only.

Thus, this legislation is intended to protect the rights of children of weaker sections studying in private and unaided schools. In addition, it restricts the fees charged by these schools from such reserved category of students to the same extent of per child expenditure incurred by the State or the actual amount charged from the child whichever is less. In spite of such welcoming provisions in this legislation, this enactment has also been criticized by certain sections of the society that it is in violation of the Fundamental Rights of the managements of private or unaided schools, that this act is not beneficial to tribal children or children of very poor economic group who pursue non-formal education and that this Act is applicable only to the children in the age group of 6-14 years and does not cover the children up to 18 years which is the stipulated age limit in the UN Convention.

**2. Right not to work**

The Child Labour (Prohibition and Regulation) Act 1986, even though did not impose hundred per cent ban on children employment, has not allowed the employment of children in certain occupations and processes which are hazardous by nature. Some of them are:

- Railways, and other means of passenger transport
- Port authorities
- Bidi making
- Carpet weaving
- Cement manufacture
- Building construction etc.

If any one employed or allowed a child to work in any of these listed fields, punishment is also provided under this legislation[12].

The 2006 Amendment to this Act widened its scope of prohibition of child labour by further disallowing the children to work as domestic servants, in dhabas (roadside restaurants), restaurants, hotels, tea sops or other recreational centers. With this Amendment, child labour has become prohibited in nearly all the sectors; if child's labour is restricted, automatically his right to education will be guaranteed.

## 3. Rights of juveniles

The term Juvenile is derived from the latin term 'Juvenis' which means young. Industrialization, urbanization, scientific and technical advances are the major culprits for the increase of juvenile delinquency. These factors are gradually dominating the other sociological and psychological factors that also cause juvenile delinquency. The growth of cities and heterogeneous populations, great mobility and fluidity, occupational and cultural variations and over-crowded conditions have given rise to new ways of living. Juveniles are effected in an unusual way by these changing conditions. In most of the cases, social deviance among children is found to have been preceded by various phases of abandonment, destitution, neglect, truancy, vagrancy, abuse and exploitation[13]. Juvenile delinquency includes, within its purview, not only delinquent juveniles but also those who are likely to come in conflict with the law[14].

The Convention on the Rights of Child (CRC) emphasizes social reintegration of child victims to the extent possible without resorting to judicial proceedings. There are certain internationally accepted procedures in connection with juvenile offenders. For example, no death sentence can be imposed on a child nor can a child be sent to an ordinary prison to be in the company of hardened criminals etc. Hence the Govt. of India, bearing in mind the CRC, The UN Minimum Standard Rules for the Administration of Juvenile Justice 1985 (The Beijing Rules), The UN Rules for the Protection of Juveniles Deprived of the Liberty (1990), has amended in 2000 the original Juvenile Justice Act 1986. This amendment was primarily intended to protect the rights of juveniles and also the rights of the children in need of care and protection. The Act highlights the responsibilities of the State to ensure that the best interests of the child are protected in all circumstances. Some important provisions of the Act 2000 are:

- No imprisonment or keeping children in police station or jails in any circumstances.

- No joint proceedings of a delinquent child with an adult person.
- Prohibition of publication of any photograph or material likely to identify the child.
- Determination of age.
- Summons procedure for quick disposal of cases.
- No juvenile in conflict with law shall be sentenced to death or life imprisonment or committed to prison in default of payment of fine or in default of furnishing security.
- Specially instructed or trained police officers have to exclusively deal with juveniles.
- Counseling of the parents or guardians of the juvenile has to be given at the time of release after admonition.
- After-care organisations for juveniles or children released from special homes are to be established for the purpose of enabling them to lead an industrious life.
- Setting up of a fund for the welfare and rehabilitation of the juvenile.

This Act deals with two basic categories of children viz., (i) Juveniles in conflict with Law (offenders); and (ii) Destitute, neglected or orphaned children in need of care and protection.

**(i) Juveniles in conflict with Law**

Juvenile Justice (JJ) Act provides for observation homes maintained either by the State or by the State under an agreement with a voluntary organisation where a juvenile in conflict with the law can be temporarily received. This Act was again amended in 2006 and makes it mandatory for each State to constitute in every district a Juvenile Justice Board within one year of the amendment and provides for a periodic review of pending cases and speed up the procedures. For those juveniles who are required to be committed by the Juvenile Justice Board for any period, there is provision for special houses in every district or group of districts for rehabilitation of juveniles in conflict with law.

The Act has provided for the kind of sentences that can be passed by the Juvenile Justice board. For example, the Board can allow the juvenile to go home after advice or admonition preceded by counseling to the parent or guardian. The Board can order the juvenile to perform community service[15]. The creation of the Juvenile Justice Board acknowledges the principle that a child should not be tried in an ordinary court of law.

**(ii) Child in need of care and protection**

J J Act defines[16] a Child in need of Care and protection as a child without home, or if resides with a person and there is a threat of killing or injury; mentally or physically challenged or suffering with incurable disease; whose parent or guardian is unfit or incapacitated to take care of the child or an orphan.

These children in need of special care can be extremely vulnerable to abuse and exploitation. We have instances of child labour or children in bonded labour often with the consent of the parents, exploitation of children for begging, for camel racing or organ trading and the like; mentally retarded children who are made to do hard work in factories by their exploiters, children trafficked for sexual exploitation and pornography, and child brides who are too young to understand and shoulder their responsibilities as a mother. There are children who are abused by their families and who run away from their homes to escape abuse and end up as street children and orphans.

The JJ Act provides for a Child Welfare Committee of lay men and women who deal with such children and also provides for the establishment of children homes to protect these children and to take care of them. The JJ Act amended in 2006 and for the first time enables such children to be given in adoption by the court in keeping with the provisions of the various guidelines for adoption issued by the State Government or by the Central Adoption Resource Agency (CARA). CARA generally provides for a home study of the adoption parents, a study of the child adopted, the health reports of the parents and the child, and appropriate safeguards for the child including a proper ascertainment of the child being available for adoption. The JJ Act further enables a person of any community or religion to adopt a child irrespective of the marital status of that person. The act has also enabled parents to adopt a child of either sex irrespective of the sex of his or her biological or existing adopted children.

In spite of various provisions and welcoming measures to protect the rights of juveniles, the said Act has also been subjected to certain criticisms by the academicians and social activists. The Act reminds mostly unimplemented, if not in letter, at least in spirit. It is also an area where the Human Rights Commission can effectively work to generate both sensitization and the will to take action on the part of the burocracy. The Act provides for the establishment of homes but unfortunately, very few states have suitable observation homes or special homes for children in conflict with law. Even the homes which exist do not have the requisite programmes or personnel trained to provide rehabilitation programmes for such juveniles.

In a number of cases, the Supreme Court also directed setting of Juvenile Justice Boards in every district to deal with the cases of juveniles separately and establishment of observation homes in every district, yet many of the states are to comply with this order. In 2007 itself, the Apex Court directed the Chief Secretaries of all states which have not filed the compliance report to personally look into the matter and respond to it within two months[17]. Another lacuna is children in conflict with law and children in need of care and protection are sent to some or similarly closed institutions resulting in deprivation of liberty. The deprivation of liberty means any form of detention or imprisonment or the placement of a person in a public or private custodial settling from which this person is not permitted to leave at will by order of any judicial administrative or public authority[18].

However, "the law relating to juveniles, both neglected and delinquent, is a part of the human rights legislation and this Act is designed to take care of, giving protection, providing treatment, development and rehabilitation of neglected and delinquent juvenile and being so, the courts must be more concerned with the colour, content and context of the legislation"[19].

## 4. National Commission

In the year 2003, Govt. of India has adopted the National Charter for Children and to implement the provisions, the Commission for the protection of Child Rights Act 2005 is enacted. This legislation provides for the constitution of a National Commission for Protection of Child Rights consisting of a chairperson who is a person of eminence and has done outstanding work for promoting the welfare of children and six members of which at least two shall be women who must be persons of eminence, ability, integrity, standing and experience in education, child health, care, welfare or child development etc[20]. Some of the functions of the Commission are:

- Enquire into the violation of child rights and recommend initiation of proceedings.
- Examine all factors that inhibit the enjoyment of rights of children effected by terrorism, communal violence, riots, natural disaster, domestic violence, HIV/AIDS, trafficking, maltreatment, torture and exploitation, pornography and prostitution and recommend appropriate remedial measures.
- Undertake and promote research in the field of Child Right
- Spread Child Rights Literacy through publication and mass media.
- Inspect Juvenile Custodial Homes or other such places where children are detained for the purpose of treatment, reformation or protection and take up remedial measures.

- Inquire into complaints and take up *suo moto* notice of matters relating to deprivation and violation of Child Rights and non-implementation of Laws providing for the protection and development of children etc.

The Commission may also move the Supreme Court or High Court for any direction or recommend the grant of interim relief to the victim or members of his family. State Commissions at State level also constituted and perform similar functions within the State. Under this Act, State Government is empowered to establish Children's Courts for the purpose of providing speedy trial of offences against children or of violation of Child Rights. The National Commission for protection of Child Rights has also been constituted and it is expected that there must be a close interference among the Commission, the State Government and the Ministry of Women and Child Development. It is therefore necessary that a coordinated effort must be made by the three agencies.

**5. Rights Against Sexual abuse**

Very recently in 2011 the Central Government cleared a Bill" Protection of Children Against Sexual Assault, Sexual Harassment and Pornography" that provides for the establishment of Special Courts for trial of such offences. Rigorous punishments are provided if the assault/harassment is committed by a person in position of trust or authority or against a child below the age of 12 years or against pornography. This Bill imposes an obligation on media, studio and photographic facilities to report the cases of pornographic exploitation of children, otherwise they will be punished[21]. To recognize the right of Privacy of Child, this Bill envisages a set of procedures for media on reporting that would bar giving personal details of the victim and the victim's family or any form of reporting that can lead to their identification. Besides it proposes Special Courts and more sensitive ways in dealing with crimes against children. This bill if enacted would cover all new aspects of sexual offences against children not covered elsewhere with stringent punishment.

## Conclusion

In recent years, our Indian Judiciary is playing a vital role in recognizing and protecting the rights of Children. In 2011, in Bachapan Bachao Andolan case[22], the Supreme Court gave decision in favour of children who are working in Circuses. The Supreme Court reiterated the importance of Children's Right of Free and Compulsory Education, Right not to Work in any hazardous occupation and the Right to have shelter in the Welfare Homes if they needed care and protection. While pronouncing the above judgment, the Apex Court said 'India is the home of 19 per cent of the world's children, that more than 1/3 of Indian population i.e., around 440 million is below 18 years and that in spite of said ratio, the total expenditure on children in India was extremely low in the years 2005-2006 and 2006-2007 ...". This reveals the lack of commitment on the part of Government on the welfare of children.

This Bachpan Bachao Andolan Case filed in the year 2006 by way of writ petition under Article 32 of the Constitution to protect the Rights of Children who are employed in Circus Companies. This Writ petition placed materials, instances of detailed forms of child exploitation, abuse and inhuman treatment of children in circuses and their forceful detention there. The petitioner explained that in spite of his best efforts and even negotiations with Indian Circus Federation (ICF), he could not stop this abuse, that how the police, Labour Department and State machinery could not come to the aid of these children.

Very fortunately the Highest Court of our Country reacted in this issue positively and gave certain directions to the Central and State Governments: They are:

- Directing the Central Government to issue suitable notification prohibiting employment of children in circuses within two months from the date of judgment.
- Government is directed to conduct simultaneous raids on all circuses to liberalize the children and check the Fundamental Rights of the children.

- The rescued children are to be kept in the Welfare Homes i.e., in the care and protection homes till they attain the age of 18 years.
- Directing that free and compulsory education has to be provided to the children who are below the age of 14 years.

Besides the Legislative protection and Judicial intervention to protect the Child Rights, children require counseling, psychological support, training and education and they need to be sensitized to their social environment, their duties and rights for their growth and Development. Then only we can expect reduction in juvenile delinquency and perfect children in our Indian Society.

## REFERENCES

1. Preamble of the 1959 Declaration on the Welfare and Protection of Child.
2. Article 1 of the Convention on the Rights of the Child 1989.
3. Law Relating to Women & Children, Mamata Rao 2ed. Eastern Book Company.
4. Srinivas Gupta: Human Rights of the Child. (1994) 7 CILR.
5. Justice Gulab Gupta: Human Rights and Fundamental Freedoms in India. M.P. Human Rights Commision, Bhopal 2002. p. 195.
6. Article 4 of the Convention on the Rights of the Child 1989.
7. Article 24 of the Convention on the Rights of the Child 1989.
8. Unnikrishnan J .P. v State of Andhra Pradesh. 1993 1 SCC 645, 730, 731.
9. 86th Amendment of Indian Constitution.
10. http://ssa.nic.in/page-portlet.links?folder name=alternative-schoolin
11. http://ssa.nic.in/news/sarva-siksha-abhiyan-in-maharashtra/
12. Sec.14 of the Act provides punishment up to one year (minimum three months) or with fine up to Rs.20,000 (minimum 10,000/- ) or with both.
13. Juvenile Justice System in India: An Appraisal. Dr. T.H. Khan. CILQ Vo. 7.1. p. 65.

14. Law and Child, R.Cambrayo & Co. Pvt. Ltd. 2004.
15. Sec.15 of Juvenile Justice Act 2006.
16. Sec.2(d) of Juvenile Justice (Care and protection) Act 2000.
17. Jameel v State of Maharashtra (2007) 11 SCC 420; AIR 2007 SC 971.
18. Rule 11 (b) of the UN Rules for Children Deprived of Liberty 1990.
19. Sarita v State (1990) SCR 86 (Bom.) 1990 Sr. L J 351.
20. Child Protection and Child Rights. http://www.child in india.org.in/child-in-india.htm visited on 21-7-2012.
21. "Cabinet Clears Child Protection Bill" – The Hindu, English Daily News Paper 4th March 2011.
22. Bachpan Bachao Andolan v Union of India and Others. (2011) 5 SCC 1.

# Child Rights and Child Labour in India

– G. Vidyavathi

The life of an individual from birth to about 16 years of age is the most crucial period in the development of personality. If parental affection, peaceful home and healthy environment are not available for children, they are subjected to bonded labour, torture, sexual abuse. Them they cannot develop mental health and harmonious personality.

Today's child is tomorrow's citizen. Children are vital resources and the most important national asset. Children need special protection and care because of their physique and tender age as well as mental immaturity and incapacity to look after themselves. Hence, it becomes so essential that they are brought up in an atmosphere of love, affection, care and attention of parents. This will help them to attain full emotional, intellectual, spiritual stability and maturity. Surveys in developing countries indicate that the vast majority of children are engaged in primary sectors such as agriculture, fishing, hunting and forestry. Eight per cent are involved in manufacturing, wholesale and retail trades, restaurants and hotels; seven per cent in domestic work and services; four per cent in transport, storage and communication; and three per cent in construction, mining and quarrying. Child labour often assumes serious proportions in commercial agriculture that is associated with global markets for cocoa, coffee, cotton, rubber, sisal, tea, etc.

India joined other nations in the observance of the first International Labour Organisations (ILO) sponsored World Day against Child Labour on 12th June 2002 with renewed determination to attack an endemic problem that is basically linked to poverty and illiteracy. Rights of children to protect from economic exploitation specifies that the state shall provide protection to children from economic exploitation and that are there to well-being.

## Nature of Child Labour

According to Child Labour Prohibition and Regulation Act, 1986, employment of children upto the age of 14 years and in case of hazardous employment up to 18 years is defined as child labour. Child labour is believed to exist at a smaller scale in the organised sector like match factories, tea factories and mica industries but a large number of children are employed in unorganised sector such as hotel industry including tea shops and way side restaurants, domestic services, carpet and metal industry. They are also employed in newspaper selling agencies.

## Causes of Child Labours

The causes of child labour are many and deep-rooted and interwoven in social and cultural heritage of Indian society it is a socio-economic problem the international labour organisation has rightly observed that child labour is essentially a problem of development it is a phenomenon deeply rooted in economic and social conditions. Some of main causes are as follows:

1. High Population Growth
   - Decreased infant mortality and increased life expectancy, more dependency burden on the earning members of the family.

- Many children produced of a couple with underlying philosophy, "Two hands to work but only one mouth to feed".
- Each member of the family is required to contribute to the family's purse.

2. Poverty is the root cause
   - Low per capita income due to large family.
   - Rise in cost of living.
   - To meet even basic necessities among masses of low socio-economic people, children are required to work
3. Lack of Schooling
   - Lack of motivation for schooling on the part of parents and children
   - Parent's attitude: "more fruitful use of time than spending on schooling"
   - Girls required taking care of house and siblings while parents work.
4. Traditional craft taught to children
   - While helping the parents, children are taught traditional craft of the parents which becomes a regular economic activity later.
5. Unemployment/Underemployment of parents
   - Death/Disease illness of earning parent forces, child is to be in the labour force.
6. Family tensions/parental apathy

   Broken homes, tension within the homes, parental rejection lead to:
   - Avoidance of schooling;
   - Necessitates earning; and
   - Running away from home, hence earn for self-survival.
7. Migrancy from villages
   - Family migration from rural to urban area hence child's work needed to supplemental family income.

- Child runs away from rural to urban areas to earn for self-support.

The following are the important rights of children included in the charter and also in the constitution of some countries like India.

1. The right to peaceful and affectionate family life.
2. Right to security of life both physical and mental.
3. Right to healthy living in healthy environment, including special treatment and care of the disabled children.
4. Right to education.
5. Right to protection-from separation of children, from parents, by illegal means, illegal adoptions, from exploitation of their labour, from discriminations due to sex, caste, colour and creed, from mental and physical torcher and from sexual abuse.

**Educational Implications of Child Rights**

For children below 9 years schools should be setup within walkable distance i.e. within a kilo meter. For children above 9 years, upper primary and secondary schools should be available within 3-5 kms. All children should be covered by these facilities. Universal enrolment and retention should be encouraged. Steps should be taken for early children care and education for children in the age group 3-6. This is necessary for creating health care prevention f disabling diseases and for creating school going habits. The government and non-governmental organisation should start courses of education like free distribution of dress, books, stationary and nutrious food.

An urgent and important step is to create awareness are children's rights among parents and community. Awareness on education programmes should be organised by the government and voluntary organisations through education institutions, mass media and other related departments like women and child welfare, youth services and health care. In developing countries children's rights are not respected mainly because of the following reasons.

- Ignorance of law regarding children's rights.
- Ignorance of the facilities created by the government and nongovernment organisations.
- Poverty.
- Negative attitude towards girl child.
- Corruption and greed of the anti social elements and some personel of the welfare departments and institutions.
- Legal cells should be opened to register and dispose of cases of violation of children's rights.

**Child Rights in India**

The convention of Rights of children came into force in 1990. India is one of the 105 countries which signed the convention. Hence, under international law India is obliged to take necessary steps for the implementation of convention. Indian as been making provision for women and child welfare in every 5-years plan. During these 5-years plan, child welfare services have been taken up which are productive, developmental and rehabilitative in nature. The following are some of the programmes.

- Supplementary nutrition.
- Immunization.
- Healeh check-up.
- Referral services.
- Nutrition and health education.
- Balwadis and anganwadis for children below 6 years of age pregnant mothers and child caring mothers in most backward rural and tribal villages and urban slums.

The Government of India has recognized the importance of voluntary organisations. Financial assistance is given to various voluntary organisations to initiate programmes related to the protection and development of children in some programmes. The voluntary and government agencies are working together. The experience in several countries has shown that activates related to health and recreation can be affectively implemented, if they are associated with education. In our country also in the 5-year plans health and child care activities are implemented through balwadis and primary schools. This practice has improved attendance in schools also non-formal education programmes have been taken up in order to help the children who cannot benefit from formal education.

The Government of India has started National Institutes for the disabled besides taking care of the blind, deaf, dumb and spastic children. These institutes train experts for the diagnosis of special education and rehabilitation. There are children's homes run by the government and also by voluntary agencies these homes protect destitute children and also give education for their development. There are also reformatories and borstal schools in order to rehabilitate child criminals.

## Identifications of Child Labour

Identification of child labour is not always easy. Therefore, the first task for the panchayats is to identify and survey the child labour situation in their respective areas. In this, all three tiers of panchayats – Zilla Parished, Panchayat Samiti and Gram Panchayats have to be involved. In addition to door –to-door visits, gram panchayats can conduct the survey in gram sahba/pallesabha meetings. These meetings are attended by all villagers who know each other. However, it is important that villagers are told about the benefits of sharing information about themselves and their children. Village level workers, youth clubs and anganwadies, etc. could be trained on child labour these people can then help panchayats by conducting the survey. After the Supreme Court judgment 196 asking surveys to be completed within six months, many bogus reports were submitted in order to beat the deadline. But with the involvement of panchayats who work directly with the people on a day- to-day basis, a credible exercise to identify child labour in the villages could be undertaken.

## Conclusion

Children are tomorrow's citizens and precious national assets-would learn to respect human rights if they are provided with fulfillment of their rights. One of the child rights is protection from exploitation, especially economic exploitation. The clear violation of this is involvement of millions of children in labour force as child labour, mostly in unpaid/low paid forms. Children are exposed to occupational hazards having serious consequence on their mental and physical development. The government has passed acts and has a special policy for children but it lacks effective enforcement machinery. There is a need to combat poverty and adult unemployment being the root cause of child labour.

## REFERENCES

Annan, Kofi, A., (1998), "Foreword", The State of World's Children, Oxford; U.K., Oxford University Press.

Gupta, M. and Klaus (1998), Course Material on Child Labour in India, New Delhi.

Singh Leena (1993), "A Profile of Working Children in India: An Overview ", in Children at Work. B.R. Publishing Corporation, New Delhi.

Talesra Hemlatha, Maneesha Shukul, Uma Shankar Sharma, Challenges of Education Technology- Trends- Globalisation.

Verma. S.B, Shiwkumar. J, Kumar Jyoti Kushwah, (2006), Rural Women Empowerment, Deep and Deep Publications, New Delhi, India.

# Child is a Blossom but not a Burden

– B.Praveena Devi

"When you look into a child eyes you expect to see hope, trust and innocence, but when you see these signs of childhood are replaced by betrayal, hunger, fear and suspicion, we need to take serious stock of ourselves and the society we have created". Nandana Reddy, opening address from the National workshop on the Rights of the child, 1988.

Child' is the sound, which brings a sense of love, affection, empathy, care etc., will come into our mind. There is no apt relation between the words child and labour. They cannot combine. Child is the future of this nation. They should sculpture at the rate of country's progress. Today, our nation is search of youth who can equalize the rupee with dollar. We should mould our child with this aspiration. To support this view, we need a media that is education. Education is the best technique which can uproot the evils existed in the society. Today, world is gazing at our nation as more than 50 per cent youth are suppose to be exist in future. Therefore, to present a skillful youth to this world what is our plan of action. First thing we should mind is - view the child as a bud but not as burden. For any one childhood is a time of fun, hope, trust, thirst of knowledge etc., but not carrying labour on their shoulders.

Indians dreaming - our nation should dictate economical boundaries to developed countries. This dream into a real picture can be done by the youth only, who are today are children. Our role to make this dream to be real picture cast the child free from all burdens and independently develops their skills and fulfills their thirst of knowledge. They should be bonded with joyful knowledge instead of forceful knowledge. Our schools curriculum, motive, importance, concentration should be on Childs career instead of materialistic things. The schools should attract the student instead of repelling the student. In this context, some approaches suggested to uproot the evils existed in the society regarding the child labour and their education.

Lasting Querries are:

- Is child a blossom or a burden
- Why do extreme poverty and misery, famines, diseases, still persist and affect so many children?
- Why do so many situations weaken and even destroy families and force children to exercise poorly paid and hazardous jobs, to steal, to be trapped into slavery or obliged to sell their body?
- Why are there so many children with no legal existence, no identity;
- Why are disabled children ignored or abandoned in so many countries?
- Why drugs and their trade which ensnare many young people with the risk of destroying them?
- Why is the right to quality education for all denied to so many children making their access into the labour market difficult and hampering their possibility to become the protagonists of their own development?

- Why financial speculation, deregulation of markets, unrestrained pursuit of profit instead of a sustainable development for all? and
- Who is the real person to mould the child labour from child? Parents, Society, financial Crisis, environmental conditions.

Can these queries come back with right path of actions. It's a doubt. Who will lead to answer all these queries - Parent, Society, administrators may be no one. But a man who is having the sense of nation development definitely think for some approaches the best is to think of some sort of approaches which can stress that child is comfortable with books, toys, friends etc., but not hand full of work. Approaches should avail the child's right to be at the door steps of the need. They may be practicable or impracticable that is second issue but let us start with a step towards it.

**Approaches**

Children have an innocent passion for life, which allows them to grow and learn with their peers. If not concealed by today's society, this positive energy will support their growth despite the numerous challenges and suffering that life inevitably carries with it.

1. The child is active but not passive. Be them active with his activities instead of passive with unwanted activities.
2. All children, are alike, without distinction of color, religion, culture, caste, creed, economic status etc.
3. The child's right to life, to survival and development capabilities should be supported.
4. The child's right to express own views freely, freedom of thought, conscience and religion and the freedom of association all should be encouraged.
5. We should aim at the integral development of the child, which goes beyond material goods and includes all dimensions, including the spiritual one.
6. The family, as the fundamental group of society and the natural environment for the growth and well-being of

all its members and particularly children, should be afforded the necessary protection and assistance so that it can fully assume its responsibilities within the community. The urgent need to protect family unit as the place capable to grant child the necessary security for his/her growth.

7. To guarantee that children become aware of other cultures without losing their history, their own culture, that is to say the resources and values upon which they have built their identity and human richness.
8. In order for the child to become a right-holder, we think that we have namely:
   - To support child resilience,
   - To encourage child participation, solidarity and responsibility,
   - Support children to find their roots and landmarks.
9. Identification to a well-defined cultural context, which structures the child identity not only from a cultural point of view, strictly speaking, but also sociologically and psychologically:
10. Allowing children to find their roots and landmarks so that their life acquires a meaning
11. Guarantee quality education to every child.
12. A mentally or physically disabled child should enjoy a full and decent life, in conditions, which ensure dignity, promote self-reliance, and facilitate the child's active participation in the community.
13. A real human ecology needs to be developed so that each human being, each child can find his/her stability and
14. Every child is intuitive bearing the note that God has not yet lost conviction in Humanity. So the human should respect the child at the rate of nations development.

### Agencies

The agencies which can practice these approaches and become a part of the child's growth are Parents, Family, Peer

Group, Society, Organisations, Administrators, NGO Groups, Educational Institutions, Teachers, Social Reformers, everyone who is a part of this nation.

- Parents and Family usually loves their children but in some cases when financial crisis arrives their blossoms becomes burden. They are supposing to plan in such a way that their children are flavors of their happiness but not a part of their budget.
- Peer Group and Society usually influence the children to think themselves as a part of earning group, it should be modified that they are future designers of the family but not the present manufacturers.
- Society, Organisations, Administrators, NGO Groups & Social Reformers, usually try to maintain the status co of the child as a blossom up to paper work but when the scenario comes to reality is different. This is may be due to some culprits in their path. So, if proper planning with good number of social workers was attested to carry the child's growth or welfare definitely child is a blossom but not a burden.
- Educational Institutions and Teachers, usually their role is to teach the children. Besides this, their role is to influence each one who is offender for child's welfare.

## Conclusion

We shouldn't think for some one's arrival for change. Change should be from our self and part of action should start from our doorstep itself. Let us hand together to bring the awareness among everyone that child is a blossom but not a burden.

## REFERENCES

Dasgupta A., R K Sen, Problems of Child Labour in India, Deep & Deep Publications, New Delhi. ISBN: 8176294268.

The Economics of Child Labour by Alessandro Cigno, Furio C. Rosati. p. 250.

# Index


**A**

Abandoned children, 27
Academic institutions, 141
African Charter on the Rights and Welfare of the Child, 77
AIDS, 10, 97
Amalinagar, 39
Annan, Kofi, 202, 204
ANOVA, 212, 213, 214, 215, 216
Anuradha, J., 144
Apex Court, 239
Apprentices Act, 1961, 18
ASMAE India Project, 35
Attitude, 188
Avenues of Child Labour, 3
Aviva, 20
Awareness of child rights, 205-220
- analysis of data, 212
- hypotheses of the study, 209-210
- interpretation of data, 212-216
- introduction, 205-207
- major findings, 217
- methodology, 210-211
- objectives of the present study, 208-209
- review of literature, 207-208

**B**

Bachpan Bachao Andolan Case, 242
Bangladesh, 135
Begging, 103
Begum, A. Jahitha, 164
Behavioural changes among children of Gandhigram crèche project and children club members Dindigul district, 32-67
- area of the study, 39
- background of the study, 36-37
- data analysis, 39
- data collection, 39
- introduction, 32-34
- major findings, 39
- methodology, 38
- objectives, 38
- other issues in India, 34-36
- suggestions, 63-65
- tools used, 38-39
- why study children, 38

Bhaskaracharyulu, Y., 170, 205
Bihar, 34
Bonded Labour System Act of 1976, 145

**C**

CACL, 108

CARA, 238
CCEA, 19
CDWs, 34
CEDAW, 80
CES, 169
Chettiapatty, 39
Child Abuse, 31
Child Act, 83
Child and a Vulture, 203
Child Development Policy, 81
Child in need of care and protection, 2 38
Child is a blossom but not a burden, 252-256
    agencies, 255-256
    approaches, 254-255
Child Labour (Prohibition and Regulation) Act, 1986, 112
Child labour a predicament of the country prosperity, 100-110
    age of the child, 102-103
    cannot we stop child labour, 105-106
    impact of child exploitation on children, 104-105
    Indian scenario of child labour and legislation, 103-104
    introduction, 100-102
    role of stakeholders in stopping child labour, 106-108
Child Labour Act, 16, 104
Child labour and street children, 1
Child Labour Prohibition and Regulation Act of 1986, 172
Child Labour Technical Advisory Committee, 17, 113
Child labour, 3-14
    classification of child labour, 6-8
    – – bonded child labour, 7
    – – child combatant, 8
    – – commercial and sexual exploitation of children, 8
    – – domestic work, 6
    – – non-domestic and non-monetary work, 6-7
    – – wage labour, 7
    concept, 4
    definition, 4-5
    government initiatives for the working children, 12-13
    harmful effects of child labour are, 8-9
    ILO's definition, 5-6
    implication of in appropriate work for children, 9-10
    introduction, 3-4
    issues of working children, 11
    problems of working children, 11-12
    reasons for child labour, 6
    street children and education, 119
Child prostitution, 29-30
Child rights and child labour in India, 245-251
    causes of child labours, 246-248
    child rights in India, 249-250
    educational implications of child rights, 248-249
    identifications of child labour, 250
    nature of child labour, 246
Child rights, 180, 199

Child trafficking, 30
Child Welfare Committee (CWC), 23
Children of the street, 27
China, 29
Christian, 40
Civil society/peoples forum, 107
CLA, 13
CLASP, 116
Cognitive development, 12
Concept of child rights, 221
Constitution of India, 111, 232
Corporate entities, 107
Corporate Social Responsibility (CSR), 140
CRC, 80, 101, 177, 236
CRIN, 178
CRRC, 108
CWIN, 135

D

Declaration of the Rights of the Child, 206
Deepthi, Kapu, 170
Democratic Republic of the Congo (DRC), 74
Devan, K., 201
Devi, B. Praveena, 252
Devi, C. Gayatri, 230
DPEP, 177
DPIP, 177

E

Education and child development, 144-149
    introduction, 144-146
    role of home, 146-148
    – – teacher, 148-149
Education and literacy, 15
Education for All, 164
Education for us, 164-169
    Chettipalayam near radio station, 167
    Kurichy road, 166
    objectives, 165
    Podanur main road, 165
    problems faced by the subjects, 167-169
    remedial measures, 169
        children education centres, 169
        mobile schools, 169
        mobile students, 169
    sample, 165-167
    teacher colony, 167
Educational Institutions and Teachers, 256
Emotional development, 12

F

Factories Act 1948, 16, 231
Factory Act of 1881, 16
Faith, 232
Fundamental Rights, 111

G

Gandhi, 36, 162
Gandhigram Creche Project, 37, 39, 50, 55
Gandhigram Rural Institute, 36
Geneva Declaration, 232
Giri, V.V., 5
God, 255
Government of India, 27
Govt. of India, 236

Gram Panchayats, 112, 250
Grant-in-Aid Committee, 233
Green Revolution, 51
GRI, 36, 50
Gurupadaswamy Committee, 16, 170

**H**

Hearing disability, 186-197
Hearing disability, 187
Hidden workers, 15
Himabindu, Goteti, 100
Hindus, 40
HIV/AIDs, 8, 10, 24, 30, 31, 35, 183
Humanity, 255

**I**

ICCPR, 232
Illiteracy, 24
ILO, 77, 100, 171, 246
Immoral Traffic (Prevention) Act 1956, 34
Indian Circus Federation, 242
Indian Constitution, 12
Indian Penal Court (IPC), 102
Individual social service activists, 107
Industrial Disputes Act, 1947, 18
International Day for Street Children, 20
International Labour Organisation, 16
IPEC, 116, 177
IRDP, 114
Issues and concerns of child labour and street children, 15-24
  child labour in India, 19-20
  department of education, 23
  introduction, 15-16
  laws about child labour, 16-18
  laws on street children, 21
  recent amendments for child labour, 18-19
  reduction of the child labour wings, 19
  street children, 20-21
    in India, 21
ITIs, 23

**J**

Jagadeeswari, V., 186
Jesudoss, C. Jim, 221
JJ Act, 238
Joshi, Uma, 133
Junior Red Cross, 51
Juvenile Justice Act, , 16236
Juveniles in conflict with law, 237

**L**

Learning disabilities, 187
Life, liberty and Pursuit of Happiness, 201
Loving and working, 73

**M**

Maternity Benefit Act, 1961, 18
Mental retardation, 187
MIGRATES, 165
Minimum Age Convention 1973, 174
Minimum Wages Act, 113
Mishra, Santosh Kumar, 68
Mizoram, 34
Mother Clubs, 148

**N**

Nachimuthu, K., 15

NAECL, 116
Narikkuravas, 168
Natarajan, V. Seeni, 25
National Child Labour Committee, 5
National Child Labour Policy (NCLP), 13, 172
National Commission, 240
National Government Agencies, 106
National Institutes, 250
National Policy of Education (NPE-1986), 13, 17, 114, 164
National Policy Resolution for Children, 233
Nehru, R.S.S., 205
NFE, 113, 142
NGO, 18, 23, 65, 69, 80, 106, 108, 134, 177, 218, 256
Nirmala, Y., 170
NLRD, 177
Nomads, 165
Non-formal education for street children, 133-143
    role of government and strategies, 140-142
    role of media, 139-140
NPC, 12
NPCL, 113, 114
NREP, 114

**O**

OC, 217
Oothupatty, 39
Operations Research Group, 5

**P**

Panchayat Samiti, 112, 250
Parent Education Association, 148
Parents, 54
Parliament Labour Laws, 18
Payment of Bonus Act, 1965, 18
Payment of Gratuity Act, 1972, 18
Payment of Wages Act, 1936, 18
Peer Group, 256
Persons with Disabilities (PWD) Act, 1995, 187
Physical development, 12
Piles of garbage, 26
Plantation Labour Act, 1951, 18
Poverty, 15, 24, 28, 75, 78, 105
Problems of child labour and education of working and street children in Chennai, 121-132
    child labour, 122
    construction of the tools and data collection, 126-127
    family size of the sample covered by the study, 127
    findings and suggestions, 129-130
    gender discrimination, 122-123
    health, 123-124
    homelessness, 124
    introduction, 121-122
    level of education of the child labourers, 128-129
    methodology, 125
    objectives of the study, 125-126
    population of the study, 126
    poverty, 124-125
    reasons for choosing work, 127-128
    -- discontinuance of education, 129

Problems of street children in Africa, 68-99
- Africa is ignoring the problem of street children, 81
- African committee of experts on the rights and welfare of the child, 94-95
- – government's response to the problem of street children, 79-81
- areas needing special attention, 93-94
- breakdown of the family and the emergence of street children, 78-79
- community response to the problem of street children, 82-83
- consequences, 76-78
- definition of street children, 69-70
- extent of problem, 71-72
- finding gainful employment to street children, 88-92
- highlights of the problem, 72-73
- introduction, 68-69
- looking into the contributing factors, 70-71
- poverty and street children in Africa, 78
- role of NGOs in addressing the problem of street children, 87-88
- selected types of community-based actions, 95-96
- strengthening the family unit, 85-87
- too little to make a difference, 81-82
- voices of street children must be heart, 92-93
- what needs to be done, 83-84
- why are children on the streets, 73-76

Problems of street children, 25-31
- categories of street children, 27
- child abuse, 30-31
- – labour, 29
- – prostitution, 29-30
- – trafficking, 30
- – /juvenile, 26
- health, 28
- homelessness, 29
- introduction, 25-26
- issues and concerns, 27
- poverty, 28
- who are street children, 26

Promoting reading habits among rural children, 150-163
- data analysis, 154-161
- data collection, 154
- hypothesis, 153
- importance of reading, 151-152
- innovative strategies, 161-162
- introduction, 151
- objectives of the study, 153
- problem faced by them, 152-153
- research methodology, 153
- research tools, 153
- sampling design, 153

**R**

Raja, L., 32, 150

Rajasthan, 34

Reddy, Nandana, 252
Rehabilitation-cum- Welfare Centres, 18
Rengasamy, T., 3
Renuka, P., 186
Respectable parent, 74
Right not to work, 235
Right of Children to Free and Compulsory Education Act, 2009, 234
Right of Juveniles, 236
Rights against sexual abuse, 241
Rights of an Indian child, 230-244
historical background, 231
Indian constitutional rights, 232-233
international concern, 231-232
introduction, 230-231
national policy, 233-234
other legislations, 234-241
Rights of children, 201-204
introduction, 201-204
Rights of Man and Citizen in 1789, 145
RLEGP, 114

S

Sarva Shikshaa Abhiyan, 23, 164, 165, 233
Say no to child labour say yes to education, 170-185
child labour eradication programmes, 177
– – legislation, 172-173
– rights, 177-179
children education, 180-182
consequences of child labour, 182-183
constitutional provisions on child labour, 173-174
convention on the rights of the child, 175
– – child labour, 174-175
introduction, 171-172
parental education, 179-180
worst forms of child labour convention, 175-176
Scarcity of schools, 24
Scheduled Caste, 164
Scheduled Tribes, 164
Self Help Groups, 227
SERP, 177
Social and moral development, 12
SOWETO, 94
Sridevi, Y., 111
Srimad Bhagavad Gita, 37
Status of child rights in India, 221-229
convention on the rights of the child, 224
history of child rights, 223-224
India signed and ratified, 224-225
introduction, 221-222
status of child rights in India, 225-227
suggestions to improve the
ensure protection of children, 227
holistic development of children, 227
promote children participation, 228
promoting child rights, 227

status of child rights in India, 227-228
what are child rights, 222-223
– – human rights, 222
– is right, 222
Strategy for eradication and elimination of child labour, 111-117
causes for child labour, 112-113
general developmental programmes, 113-116
identification of child labour, 112
international labour organisations, 116-117
legislative action plan, 113
national authority for elimination of child labour, 1994, 116
Street Child, 26, 71
Sundharavadivel, G., 121
Suryanarayana, N.V.S., 100

**T**

Teacher attitude towards inclusion of children with hearing disability, 186-197
analysis and interpretation, 191-196
Andrew, W., 189
educational implications, 197
findings, 196
hypotheses, 190
introduction, 187-188
Jones, Haward, 189
need of the study, 188
objectives, 189
review of the literature, 188-189
sample of the study, 190
Smith, A., 189
statistical techniques, 191
tools used in the study, 190
Teachers, 59
Thoppampatty, 39
TPEC, 177
TV, 56

**U**

Uganda Africa Foundation, 88
Ulagampatty, 39
UN agencies, 90
UNDP, 136
UNESCO, 137
UNICEF, 4, 21, 32, 69, 77, 80, 106, 121, 180, 201
UNIFEMs, 34
Union Constitution, 83
Union Welfare Ministry, 21
United Nations and International Labour Organisation, 16
United Nations Convention on the Rights of the Child (UNCRC), 4, 26, 31, 201, 224, 225
Universal Declaration of Human Rights (UDHR), 145, 223
Universalisation of Elementary Education (UEE), 165
UNO, 223
Unprotected, 75
Urban civilization, 73
Uttar Pradesh, 34

**V**

Vidhyanathan, S., 201
Vidyavathi, G., 245

W

Watoto wa mitaani, 74
WHO, 30
Workmen Compensation Act, 1923, 18
World Children Organisation, 32
World Conference on Human Rights 1993, 232
World War I, 223
World War II, 223

Z

Zilla Parishad, 112, 250